BETWEEN *Two* FATHERS

by Charles Barg M.D.

Purple Pomegranate Productions
San Francisco, CA

D0176530

© Copyright 2002, Purple Pomegranate Productions
Edited by Ruth Rosen
Editorial assistance by Suzanne Stone and Naomi Rose Rothstein
Cover design by Daniela Meyer

All rights reserved. Nothing in this book shall be reprinted or reproduced, electronically or in any manner, without express written permission. For more information write to:

Reprint Permissions
Purple Pomegranate Productions
60 Haight Street, San Francisco, CA 94102

ISBN: 1-881022-12-9 (pbk.)

03 04 10 9 8 7 6 5 4 3

All Scripture quoted, unless otherwise noted, is from the Holy Bible, New King James Version. Copyright 1979, 1980, 1982, Thomas Nelson Publishers. Used by permission.
Purple Pomegranate Productions is a division of Jews for Jesus®

CONTENTS

DEDICATION

This book is dedicated especially to Linda, my beloved wife for life, and to our children and grandchildren:

Paul Guinn	Christi Barg
Alison Guinn	Lauren Guinn
Sam Barg	Margot-Lindsay Guinn
Margot Barg	Caroline Guinn
Joshua Barg	

It is also dedicated to our future generations, at this time known only to God.

My very special thanks are due my daughter Margot Barg, who is both a daughter in life and a sister in the faith. Thank you, Margot, for your loving contributions of time and assistance on this work.

PROLOGUE

Sitting beside Dad as we drove along U.S. Highway 61 from Cairo to Kankakee to Chicago, my imagination soared. Someday I was going to be just like Dad! One day I'd take his place as a *gonsa macher*, the "big shot" patriarch of our large extended family. Everybody would seek me out to deal with whatever problems life could deliver, knowing full well that I would have all the answers and all the resources to carry out all the solutions.

In other words, Dad was going to teach me to be just like him, in every way.

He told me so!

I was Dad's student, traveling companion, employee, and later in life, manager of his medical care. I alternately enjoyed him, quarreled with him, deeply resented him and loved him beyond belief. In his final years, I reversed roles with him.

Dad often told me stories from his past. Somehow, he always seemed to emerge the hero. It took some time for me to figure out that at least some of these stories were somewhat exaggerated to show off his virtues in contrast to his foil (whoever else happened to share a role in the story). That, I think, was common among the storytelling of that era, or of any other for that matter.

By the time Dad died in 1997, I had begun to understand and accept his flaws and failures. I had also begun to realize that I have many aspects of his personality concealed, unnoticed, within my own self. They seem to emerge—sometimes to my discomfort and sometimes to my delight—all the more with each passing year.

Many years ago, Solomon noted, " . . . *the glory of children is their father*" (Proverbs 17:6). That same *glory* is able to either give life or to take it away. A father is always doing one or the other—giving life to his son or removing it—there are no in-betweens. As is true in my own experience, fathers are a powerful presence for good or for ill in the lives of their sons. But there is something even more powerful . . .

Louis Barg

CHAPTER ONE:

BAD MAZEL

"We never should have named him Charlie!"

It seemed that what my dad intended for blessing had turned to bad luck.

Upon entering into this world in 1943, I was named after my dead uncle. Uncle Charlie had been conceived in the "Old Country," but he was born in the "New Country" just days after his teenaged parents reached America. They arrived in New York harbor amidst a boatload of Lithuanian Jews fleeing forced conscription into the czar's army, a ten-year obligation that many Jews did not survive. For those who did manage to survive the army, there remained the ever-present threat of *pogroms*. In the early 1900s, no Jewish *shtetl* (settlement) was safe from these sudden and vicious attacks, which were driven by hatred and fueled by myth. One particularly pernicious lie was used to justify many pogroms: that the "Christ-killing" Jews plotted to use the blood of Christian children to prepare their ceremonial food and to conduct ritual sacrifices to their God.

Somehow, Israel and Rebecca Schneider escaped from Lithuania and arrived in Forrest City, Arkansas, after briefly residing in the Lower East Side of New York, then Cincinnati, Memphis, and Little Rock. Forrest City is a small southern town named after the irrepressible Confederate General, Nathan Bedford Forrest. By the time Israel and Rebecca reached Forrest City, they'd had two more children, Reuben and Golda Leah (my mother). Their hearts were filled with hope for a good and peaceful life.

Despite the overwhelmingly Gentile majority, there were just enough

1

Jewish families—fourteen or so—to continue the Jewish traditions and social life they had known. Grandpa Schneider (now Snyder) experienced more financial prosperity and respect than he had ever dreamed! Yet there was also sorrow and disappointment.

By the mid-1930s, the community noticed that Grandpa Snyder's first-born son Charlie—who'd always been known as "good old Charlie"—just wasn't himself. Charlie was a dapper, good-natured, young man who never treated anyone like a stranger. He was never more than a phone call away from a party. His natural ability to buy and sell merchandise made him an asset to his father's company.

Because he was such a spectacular salesman, Charlie's father expected him to use his skills seven days a week, which was not exactly Charlie's way of defining life. Charlie couldn't shake the feeling that he never quite measured up to his father's expectations, so he tried to drown the feeling by drinking—a lot.

After Charlie's wife left him and took their only child back to her hometown of St. Louis, he became increasingly despondent. His dress and demeanor soon became unkempt, sloppy. He seldom spoke and when he did, his voice was empty of emotion. He rarely came out of his room (he'd returned to live at his parents' home), except to eat or walk the three blocks to the liquor store. One morning, he slipped into the bathroom and fired a 38-caliber bullet into his right temple. Hardly anyone, except his parents, was surprised.

I was born five years later. In the Jewish tradition, it is unlawful to name a child after one who has taken his own life; it is considered *tsuris* (trouble) and bad *mazel* (luck). This is particularly true for the *kohanim*, the priestly order to which my grandfather belonged by virtue of birthright. Nevertheless, Dad—seeing the lingering pain of his new in-laws—insisted on naming me Charles. He hoped that new life, a fresh life, named for their son would in some way allay their grief.

I am told that it did! I was the apple of my grandparents' eyes from the day I was born. My first four years were spent under their roof while Dad was off serving in the war effort. Grandpa began shortening his long workdays in order to come home and be with me, tease me in Yiddish and take me out for an ice cream cone almost every night. We would go for long rides in his old Chevrolet, and even longer walks, as measured by time rather than miles. He often sang old Yiddish songs to me, songs from his youth. My southern drawl was flavored with a Yiddish accent for the first few years of my life.

I'm told his disposition was usually rather stern—all business—but that's not the Grandpa Snyder I remember. Grandpa was full of laughter, hide-and-seek and adventure. Everywhere we went, he took delight in showing off his grandson. His longtime Jewish friends were glad to see the joy of life return to him. For four years, he was my "father."

Then one day, I awoke to find a six-foot tall, blonde-haired, blue-eyed U.S. Marine in uniform standing over my bed. That is my first recollection of Dad; it is a grand remembrance! He was glorious and embodied all that a little boy might imagine about manhood—strength, self-assurance, stature, wisdom, energy and zeal for life. He was each of these, tempered with a certain gentleness of spirit. That was my Dad! I was in awe of him that morning, but we quickly became friends. Within a few months—in the wake of a near fatal accident—we were inseparable.

Those were the days before refrigerators, so everyone bought block ice from the corner icehouse. One spring afternoon, I stealthily climbed up to the fifth shelf in the pantry behind the kitchen where I had seen my grandmother hide the ice pick. Sneaking it out to the backyard to "work" on the front tire of my tricycle, I turned the ice pick upside down and began striking the tire with the wooden handle. Striking away, I accidentally bounced the rusty, pointed tip into my left eye. My screams from the backyard alerted Grandma. She ran outside and found me cowering behind the garage with a bleeding eye, terrified that my disobedience would be discovered.

The local general practice doctor assured my parents that the eye was only inflamed and would heal in a few days. Three days later, I had a high fever and a bulging eye, swollen shut from infection. Dad took me to the old Memphis Eye, Ear, Nose & Throat Clinic to see Carl Reichner, who was considered the best eye surgeon around. He said we had waited too long. Without surgery, the infection would likely continue on its destructive path and travel across the optic nerve to the unaffected eye, leaving bilateral blindness in its wake. Worse, it could very well lead to a brain abscess, which would surely be fatal.

For weeks the medical team fought to save my left eye, but the infection kept spreading. The doctor advised removing it, and they eventually did. One week after surgery, it became obvious the infection was going to reach across to my remaining eye. I was slowly going blind.

One day, Dr. Reichner burst into the hospital room proclaiming, "The army has a new staphylococcal-fighting antibiotic used for battlefield wounds. I have just arranged to have one of these new drugs flown to Memphis from Walter Reed Hospital in Washington, and I believe it will arrest the infection!" Thankfully, he was right and the vision in my remaining eye was restored.

Nevertheless, my parents were beset with guilt for naming me after my uncle who had killed himself. They reasoned that because Uncle Charles had a lifelong weak left eye, my mishap must have been caused by bad *mazel*, (bad luck.) For Mom, who was pregnant with my sister Barbara, dreadful memories of her brother's tragic death came flooding back. Her doctor ordered absolute bed rest to protect her and the baby, which is why the incident became such a time of bonding for my father and me. Up until then, my mother and Grandpa Snyder had seen to all my needs.

My mother was the baby of her family, and was always much protected and looked after. She had almost died at birth herself, her mother having been very ill. Mother's intelligence and charm, combined with a musical flair, was a source of delight to the family, as were her childhood dreams of becoming a dancer. However, a roller skating accident when she was twelve set up a chronic, unrelenting osteomyelitis (bone infection) in her hip.

At age eighteen, instead of going off to college with her chums, she had to go to St. Louis where she underwent surgery. She lived in a body cast in an old post-WWI orthopedic hospital for 12 months. She had no windows in her room, so she did not see sun, earth, sky, grass, trees or flowers for a year. When her dad finally brought her home, it was springtime. Mother stopped just outside the door, sat on the steps and wept because of the beauty that surrounded her.

Mom was very southern for a Jewish girl. She spent a lot of time with her cousins in the Mississippi Delta. She was also popular and well received by the Gentile aristocracy in Forrest City. Her parents spoke primarily Yiddish, but they encouraged their daughter in the ways of old time genteel southern culture. She always had one or two " maids" and "cooks" helping her out after she was married, as her mother convinced her she shouldn't try to take on too much. Dad protected her from stress and strain throughout their lives together, and my accident in the midst of her difficult pregnancy was a case in point.

With Mother virtually incapacitated, Dad set aside his work and career goals to stay at my bedside and care for me. Every minute of every day, he was there encouraging me and cheering me on, understanding my fears and constantly assuring me that he would never leave me alone in the hospital. He would sit me on his lap in the rocking chair and read me stories, or tell me his war stories. Then he would say, "Everything is going to be all right, son. Your life is going to be normal, and you'll still be like every other little boy."

These words came from the lips of a man who, just six months earlier, I had never met. I came to love and trust him there in that hospital ward. For several months, it was just Dad and me!

I don't know how we chiseled ice for our home after that episode because I don't remember ever seeing another ice pick in our home. In fact, I cannot think of any family member who even dared to use that word in the presence of my grandmother. They would just give "the look" and say something like, "Honey, would you please go get the . . . hmmm . . . and get some ice for dinner."

Nevertheless, without the time alone together in the hospital, Dad and I would have missed that important bonding opportunity. After returning from the war in the Pacific, Dad had joined his father-in-law and brother-in-law in a business that required 18-20 hour days on the road. Probably, if Mother had been well enough to care for me, I would not have known Dad's softer, nurturing side the way I know it today.

A boy needs to be with his father. And Dad, whose only fear in life was that he might suddenly leave this world without totally equipping me for life, wanted to be with his son. He "needed" to impart his religion, his social passions and his wealth to me. Our time together in that Memphis hospital was the beginning of a curious partnership.

CHAPTER TWO:

THE PEACEMAKER

"Momma, why is Dad going into that big building?" I asked.

Mom answered quickly, explaining that the huge granite edifice with the American flag and countless steps was some kind of Marine Corps complex where Dad had a business appointment. Dad always took a detour there whenever we headed up north to Chicago. Many years later, I discovered that the building was actually Leavenworth Federal Penitentiary, where Dad would stop to visit his older brother Jack.

My father was no stranger to visiting prisons. The Barg children, along with their stepbrothers and stepsisters had received their "education" on the mean streets of Chicago's poorer ethnic Jewish neighborhoods. Two sons were hoodlums from the mob-ridden, West Side of Chicago of the 1920s and 30s, and they spent a good part of their lives incarcerated in Joliet Federal Penitentiary with the likes of Al Capone. Thus, as a youth, Dad spent many Sundays motoring his mother to prison to visit her boys.

My father, Louis, was the youngest of Bella Barg's eleven children. For whatever reason, he was "appointed" from birth to keep peace within the family. Indeed, his mother departed this earth pleading with him to remember what she somehow considered his lifelong responsibility: to look after his errant brothers and to provide for his sisters. He had been groomed for this mission from early childhood—a mission that, by the way, was impossible.

"Peace" is the last word that comes to mind when I consider the dynamics of the Barg-Ruff clan. I am told Bella Barg's first marriage was

7

to an irresponsible, work-brittle fellow from the "old country" named Ruff. He packed up and left her in Eastern Europe with five children and a promise that he would send for them after he found work in America. When she didn't hear from him for a few years, she took the children and worked her way through Poland, Germany, France, Britain and America as a domestic housekeeper. She finally found her husband in Canada, "salooning-around" with some worthless fellows. For a few years, she tried to make the marriage work; they even had more children. However, times were very hard, and she left him before he could squander the rest of what little money they had.

Bella returned to America and began managing a rooming house in Cleveland. Before long, she met and married Shmuel (Sam) Barg, a young man just arrived from Kiev in the Ukraine. Unknowingly, they had both left Eastern Europe at the perfect time. One generation later, the Nazis targeted Jews from Lithuania and the Ukraine for total extermination. Like countless other Jewish families, our family also had relatives who had remained there and were sent off to the death camps.

Sam was quite a talker, but he never spoke of his mother and seldom mentioned his father. I suspect his mother may have been a victim of a *pogrom*, although there is no way to be certain one hundred years after the fact. Sam was eighteen years younger than his wife Bella, an extremely strong-willed woman who acted as a wife/mother to him. Sam loved his family and rose early in the morning to make a living for them. He reared Bella's children as his own and never used the word "stepchildren." Together, he and Bella had three children of their own. Louis, my dad, was the last of the line.

Dad was the only one of the 11 children to finish grade school; nevertheless he had to drop out of the eighth grade to help the family during the Great Depression. Grandpa Barg wanted to educate the children according to the traditions and piety of old country, Orthodox Judaism, but he became increasingly accommodating to local societal influences that were not exactly in accordance with rabbinic teachings. He worked hard seven days a week, drank considerably and whenever challenged, never backed down from a good fistfight. His sons, who often fought alongside him, claimed that they never saw him "get whipped."

Grandpa Barg was huge, strong and fearless. Once, while he was peddling fruit and vegetables from his horse-drawn wagon, a robber tried to threaten him with a knife. Grandpa jumped off the wagon, beat the young thug senseless, and climbed back onto his wagon more confident than ever. Figuring that the robber had learned his lesson, my grandpa never even considered having him arrested.

Two of Dad's brothers were World War I heroes. The first, Dave Ruff, is recorded in history as the hero of the Battle of Belleau Wood in France. The second, little Leo Ruff, achieved recognition as the youngest soldier to serve in that war. After stowing away in a soldier's gear bag, he had arrived in Europe on the western front lines at age twelve. He was issued a rifle and rations, and he served honorably there until the end of the war.

Three other brothers were also well known, but in a rather notorious way. They each went to prison for various crimes, including armed robbery, racketeering, counterfeiting and other such felonies. Uncle Joe, a golden gloves champion, was a cellmate to Nathan Leopold of the infamous Leopold and Loeb thrill-killing murder case in the 1920s. Joe was small, but his fists were fast and dangerous. Most of the other inmates feared his right hook, which only traveled about four inches, but was launched with surprising fury by Joe's powerful shoulder and equally powerful forearm strength. It always took his opponents by surprise. The warden once called my grandmother and told her to come to Joliet Prison immediately because Joe was fighting with everyone and could not be controlled. Dad, who was only thirteen at the time, drove her out to the prison. She met with Joe and asked him about his conduct.

"Momma," he said, "I'm one of the youngest inmates here, and you know what old cons do to young boys. Everybody thinks I'm crazy, and I want to keep them thinking that way!" She left there comforted that he was going to be all right.

Joe and Jack were always fighting. When they couldn't find anyone else to fight, they fought each other, sometimes bringing other brothers and sisters into the fray.

Once, in the 1960s at a family wedding in Natchez, Jack got drunk and threw a full bottle of liquor at Dad's head. Dad, who was chatting with a group of people on the other side of the room, was completely unaware that there was even a problem. Another brother yelled at Dad just in time. Dad looked up and caught the bottle in mid-flight, spraining his hand. Though he was the youngest, Dad was the biggest and strongest of the clan. He could have done some real damage to Uncle Jack; instead, he picked Jack up like a toy, carried him upstairs to a hotel room, then stood between Jack and the door. As Jack continued trying to punch Dad, Dad's quick reflexes and athleticism kept the blows from finding their mark until the police arrived.

Dad never could go against his brothers and sisters, no matter what they did. Many felt that it would have been better for everyone if Dad had forsaken his promises to his departed mother and let people like Jack experience the full consequences of their choices. He never did though, and everybody knew he never would.

So Jack spent a lot of time in prison during the days of the old Arkansas system, a system that was corrupt to the core—particularly under the experimental "trustee model" program. Some prisoners were employed as guards, and they were often much more brutal and corrupt than regular guards. Dad visited Jack twice a month and brought money, food and anything else that Jack could use as bribes. If Dad ever questioned the amount of money needed to keep Jack "healthy," the warden's office would call Dad and say, "We're sorry. Jack can't have visitors this week. He's in the infirmary with a sore throat." That meant that the guards had beaten Jack with rubber hoses once again, or had him on the "Tucker Telephone," a hand crank generator that activated wires hooked to a prisoner's genitals.

Jack, who had been in reform schools and prisons since age seven, didn't seem too worried; his vow was to never give up. He once told me, "Even if you're feeling bad pain, eventually you black out and feel nothing." With that kind of attitude, who can scare you? But the warden used to tell Dad, "Jack isn't doing time here, his family is doing it for him. You guys bring him anything he needs, and he's a kingpin around here."

The whole family was relieved when Jack was paroled for the last time. Dad brought him to Forrest City and taught him the steel business. Jack eventually moved to Little Rock and became quite successful in legitimate business, although, to the delight of his more shameless compatriots, he always maintained a "special" west Chicago way of doing business.

My father often shared these stories with me. Handing down stories from generation to generation is the Jewish equivalent of an afterlife. One of Dad's greatest fears was departing this earth without letting me know how it "used to be."

CHAPTER THREE:

UNCOMMON VALOR

"Chiney's got a gun and he's fixin' to kill Cross!" the voice on the other end of the phone exclaimed.

Without hesitation, Dad replied, "I'll be right there." He tossed the phone aside, swept me up with one arm and ran for the car parked in the alleyway behind the store. As we raced toward the receding light of dusk, Dad spoke softly to me, with scarcely a hint of the deep concern that must have filled his mind at that moment. "Son, it's going to be alright. There's a little problem down at the yard. I'll go and talk to Chiney and everything will be okay."

Chiney Jones was the night watchman at the old storage yard. When he was sober, which was seldom, he did a fair job of looking after things. He and his family of six lived in a two room "shotgun shack" with outdoor plumbing on the back edge of the twenty-five acre scrap yard. Small and wiry, he smelled awfully bad. He liked to drink and when he drank he was "low mean." He beat his wife and children. He hated black folks and frequently reminded them that he thought "their place" in the South began and ended at the lowest end of the food chain. His sole claim to significance came by way of the 18-inch flashlight, carried in the back pocket of his overalls and a .45-caliber, automatic weapon that swung from his hip, both of which were brought to him each evening near dark and reclaimed at daybreak the following morning.

Theodis "Sonny Cross" Warren was a young black man about twenty years old. Cross had been abandoned by his parents as a child, and he was mostly raised by his loving grandmother. He was handsome, muscular and energetic.

When Dad came home from the war, he hit the highway each morning before dawn in a three-quarter ton truck to buy merchandise, including scrap iron, metals, animal hides, furs, pecans and anything else that would sell. Dad was "the best" at finding something valuable, buying it at low cost and making a large profit. Sonny Cross was his right-hand man—and more than that, he was like family.

Cross, who never went beyond the third grade and was illiterate, could go anywhere in the central United States by simply picturing the route, if someone gave him good directions. Dad was peerless at giving good directions. Cross and Dad drove from town to town throughout the Arkansas and Mississippi River delta buying merchandise, loading it up, bringing it home and quickly warehousing and inventorying everything. They would be back on the road again before daybreak to beat the competition to the next "buy."

Driving along the highway late one rainy night and fighting to stay awake, Dad and Cross missed a tight turn onto a one-lane bridge. With 20,000 pounds of pecans chasing the front cab they narrowly missed plumbing the depths of the White River. Having stopped close to the river's edge to check if the load was still aboard, they took advantage of their immobility and napped until the wrecker arrived.

Although Cross never made a lot of money, his wife was a schoolteacher and together they did well in comparison with others in the African-American community of that day. Cross carried himself with a certain genteel dignity, which disgruntled people of Chiney's fabric. Consequently, Chiney looked for opportunities to "fix" Cross once and for all.

On one particular summer evening, Chiney was determined to resolve his problem with Cross—permanently. As Dad turned across the old railroad spur beside the night watchman's shed, I saw Chiney pressing his .45-caliber firmly against the flesh of Cross's forehead. Dad pulled to a stop, opened his door and whispered to me, "Don't make a sound, it's alright." He eased out of the car and slowly moved toward Chiney and Cross. Disobeying Dad's instructions, I moved over to the driver's side of the car, raised my head to window level and peered out to watch the developing drama.

"Get away from here Mr. Louis, I'm gonna kill this *nigger* tonight!" Chiney said.

Dad moved slowly toward them. Keeping his voice calm and deliberate he said, "Chiney, give me the gun. You're not going to shoot anyone."

Even as a five-year-old, I knew this was deadly danger. Why didn't Dad get back in the car and flee? Wasn't he as frightened as I was? I gripped the open window frame, as if somehow the force of my hands could empower Dad to overcome this dark figure. "Please God, don't let my father die," I pleaded silently.

By now, Dad had reached Cross, who was pinned against the wall of the shed. Without a trace of hesitation, Dad took a long step and positioned himself in front of Cross. Chiney's pistol was now directly against Dad's forehead and Cross stood shivering behind him. Reaching forward, Dad wrapped his large right hand around the gun barrel. Chiney tried to raise his voice to intimidate Dad, but his voice could not hide his increasing fear as he realized that he was up against someone who was accustomed to looking danger in the face and standing firm.

"Chiney, let go of the gun. If you want to shoot him, you've got to shoot me first!" Dad's voice was calm, his face like flint.

That moment was the first authentic act of sober bravery that Chiney had ever witnessed in another human being. His mouth dropped open as he released his grasp on the gun and began to weep. Reaching forward again, Dad grasped Chiney by the throat, lifted him off his feet as though he was weightless, and pinned him against the same wall where Chiney had just pinned Cross. He drew his fist back and he was ready to put Chiney's lights out for the night. His fist poised, he hesitated. Then Dad gathered himself and corralled his emotions, a phenomenon I witnessed throughout his life. After what must have seemed like an eternity to Chiney, Dad lowered his fist and relaxed his grip on the now terrified little bully. His legs were starting to give way and he nearly fainted as he slumped to the ground in a whimpering heap.

Throughout Dad's lifetime, he never backed away from doing what he thought was right. He did not invite conflict; he was, in fact, the consummate peacemaker. But when people in distress needed someone to stand up for them, my father was the first man that they called. He had uncommon valor and never retreated when he thought right was on his side.

CHAPTER FOUR:

TO "AIR" IS HUMAN

"Clear prop!" The hand crank that spooled up the engine was removed.
"Starter!" Dad hit the starter button.

"Hot mag." The magneto switch was turned to the both position. With a resounding scream, the old 220-horsepower, Continental engine on the pre-WWII Steerman jumped to life. The engine's initial scream soon metamorphosed into a deep, pulsating "lub-dub-ka" that shook the surrounding earth.

In the early post-war years, Dad had taken advantage of the 1946 GI Bill, which allowed veterans to become flyers at almost no personal expense. When Dad first heard that Japan had attacked Pearl Harbor, he drove straight to the U.S. Army induction center to enlist in the Army Air Corps. However, having almost no education, he scored two points shy of being accepted into the program. Undeterred and anxious to be in the midst of the battle, he enlisted in the U.S. Marine Corps. Like every Marine I have ever met, he remained a Marine for the rest of his life.

During boot camp at the old Santa Margarita Ranch in Oceanside, California, Dad and several hundred other Marines beat down the desert vegetation to build and populate what is now known as Camp Pendleton. After basic training, he shipped out to the Pacific maelstrom that was Guam, Tinian and Saipan. The consummate "leatherneck," he quickly attained a sergeant's ranking.

He pretty well wore out the jungles of the Marianna islands, except for occasional brief interludes of R & R back in Hilo, Hawaii. But R & R was rare because the U.S. was fighting hard to overcome Japan's considerable momentum.

After the war, Dad returned to Forrest City. He and all of the other aviation vets sought out each other's company. They had at least one thing in common—winning the war! Every Saturday morning, amidst the sounds of droning engines, these young aviators sat and drank coffee while swapping tales of glory. Cigar smoke filled the air. They proudly wore their wartime khaki and leather, stained and scented by aviation fuel, the patches on their sleeves proclaiming silent stories of previous wartime experiences. They would pat my head and call me "Louis's boy" and "little soldier." I liked that.

One particular morning in 1948, I stood alongside the airfield watching Dad s-turn the old biplane onto the path that had been cut out of the kudzu on the worn grass airstrip that was "Aycock's Field." He taxied into position for the engine run-up before take-off. Easing the throttle forward from the rear pilot's seat, open cockpit configuration, he waited as the old war bird gathered momentum and attempted to go airborne. Suddenly, it began weaving as if out of control. Quickly out of runway, the plane was still just under normal rotation speed as Dad nursed it into the air. It lifted off the sod surface . . . up . . . up . . . before it suddenly lost lift, turned earthward, nearly vertical and then nose-dived into the ground.

I was screaming and racing down the runway. The smoke was thick as I cried out, "Dad! Dad!" Someone grabbed me to prevent me from being caught in an explosion. I struggled to move forward, but strong arms were holding me back. I turned around to see that it was Dad restraining me! He was okay except for a few scratches and a torn jacket.

Grinning, he said, "Please don't tell your mother about this. She won't understand." Of course, I could not wait to tell Mom. Dad was right; she did not even begin to understand! The incident almost put an end to his flying career.

* * *

Steerman airplanes were great old airplanes, slow, double-winged planes, real maneuverable. Dad used to sit me on a cushion he'd placed over the parachutes and I'd ride in front of him. He'd bank away from the sun and we'd go out over the farms and rivers and fields and just soar. It was thrilling. I loved the smell of the aviation gas, the khaki leather gear, the cigar smoke.

Dad used his flying skills for both business and B'nai B'rith, the latter an international, Jewish philanthropic organization. B'nai B'rith was one of his greatest passions. Through this great collective body of Jewish people, my father earned recognition and respect among the "sons of Abraham." He became a local, regional, and eventually an international representative for this organization that enjoys powerful, worldwide influence in Jewish affairs. In 40 years, I don't think Dad ever missed a regional convention. When word spread that he was soaring about the countryside in his own airplane, championing various Jewish causes and campaigns, Dad's compatriots began affectionately referring to him as the "Flying Jew."

Few paved airstrips existed in the early days of Arkansas aviation. From grass airstrips out in the middle of nowhere, Dad never hesitated to have a go at a short-field takeoff, despite challenging crosswind conditions and 50-foot obstacles, such as power lines and tall trees. Onlookers always scratched their heads in disbelief. Those of us who knew Dad understood that this confirmed his self-perception of personal invincibility. He worried a lot about others, but he never showed anxiety or doubt about himself.

Dad did not put much stock in instrument flying or the study of meteorology. Once, while flying through the clouds over the Arkansas River, we were low on fuel and there was no airport in sight. I was 10 or 11 and did not know enough to be scared. Besides, everything Dad did seemed to turn out alright. I had supreme confidence in him.

Staring at the artificial horizon instrument to keep the wings level, he seemed calm. However, the voice from the control tower at Adam's Field in Little Rock was not so calm. It desperately attempted to confirm our position through high-powered field glasses so that someone in the tower could turn us safely onto runway "One-Eight." Meanwhile, unbeknownst to us, we were flying over three bridges whose arches were within 25 feet of our landing gear. At the last second, I spotted the flash of the beacon light blinking faintly through the overcast. "Dad! Look over there!" I yelled above the noise of the plane as I pointed at the light. We turned blindly toward it and landed safely once again.

Later, Dad admitted that it had been a close call. And there were others.

The close calls never prevented me from wanting to fly again, not when I was a child, anyway.

I was twenty when I developed a fear of flying. It was 1963. Dad and I had gone to Washington, D.C. for a gala event. As we were flying back (on a commercial airline), one of our engines caught on fire. We tried to make an emergency landing in Knoxville—a real mountainous town—in zero visibility and snow, as I recall. The pilot missed the approach. Obviously we survived the somewhat traumatic landing. I figured I was going to die on that airplane.

Twenty years later, when I flew my own plane across the country for the first time, I was still fighting the fear. Some people say fear is another side of anger. In any case, I did not want to be controlled by fear, so whenever I was afraid of something, I'd work through it and then just go do it.

I remember the day I was 30 miles west of Forrest City, descending, nice and smooth. However, there was not a cloud in the sky and that usually means there's a lot of wind up there. When I got down to about 5,000 feet, the air got choppy and started throwing the airplane around. It wasn't dangerous, but I had never experienced such a bumpy flight, much less on my own. I hyperventilated, my hands got heavy and then I was out. I'd fainted. I was flying solo with no auto pilot.

Before I passed out, I recollect thinking something to the effect of, "This is an ignominious way to die. I want to die doing something important." I struggled back to consciousness and landed my plane. My first response was to call Little Rock and ask them to send a couple of people and a plane. I was not flying myself back. Then I saw a fellow sitting in the hanger, a crop duster. He was chewing on a straw, leaning back in his chair—and looking at me as though I didn't belong there. He didn't talk much, but I realized that if I didn't get back into that airplane, he'd be right, I wouldn't belong there because I'd never fly again.

I went back out to the plane, kicked the tires a couple of times, turned the prop, and I was off. I was scared all the way back, but I fought the fear. That was about 1983. From there I went on and became a commercial pilot. I ended up doing spins and teaching people instruments. Now I'm just as comfortable flying under a hood in zero visibility as I would be with full visibility. I knew I couldn't give way to fear and it paid off.

Dad, on the other hand, seemed fearless. To him, close calls were simply part of life. Rather than fearing them, we were supposed to accept them and be thankful for a good outcome.

Dad flew nearly everywhere, particularly in the South and Midwest. He piloted sea planes off Navy Pier in Chicago, experienced tail dragger thrills in Natchez and hosted comedian Georgie Jessel aboard his Cessna 205 as they adventured across the Texas Rio Grande Valley "in the clouds most of the way." He logged some DC-3 "Goonie Bird" time across Israel, and once made an emergency landing due to engine fuel starvation in a rice paddy near Yazoo City, Mississippi. Another time, he mistakenly wandered over the prohibited Oak Ridge, Tennessee nuclear facility. The nuclear boys scrambled two jet fighters to escort him to earth and examine his intentions.

Time and space do not permit a complete recounting of all of Dad's airplane adventures. They filled my boyish imagination with dreams of adventure and glory. When I would share these tales of Dad "slipping the surly bonds of earth" among my buddies, they were filled with admiration for him—and he was my father!

CHAPTER FIVE:

THAT OLD TIME RELIGION

"I can't wait at home for Barry and Shelly, Grandma. I'm going to be saved tonight!"

I could not contain my excitement as I peeked out the window to see if anyone was arriving at the big yellow canvas tent erected across the street in City Park. It was summertime in 1950, and Grandma wanted me home when our cousins from Chicago arrived. But I had other plans.

I was staring out the kitchen window of Grandpa Snyder's house. He had built it in the late 1920s, after his wooden frame house—built on the same site—burned to the ground. Like other southern homes built before the arrival of air conditioners, Grandpa Snyder's fine home had high ceilings, window awnings, an attic fan that lulled everyone to sleep at night and a screened-in sleeping porch. In the big backyard, there were tall, stately oak trees and bushy shrubbery with branches hanging so close to the windows that I could reach out and touch them.

This was the home in which I grew up. Forrest City was a quiet little community of about 12,000. Folks called it "the hub of eastern Arkansas." It is nestled in Crowley's Ridge, a small rise in the north-south earth that stretches from its southern border of Helena on the Mississippi River, to somewhere up in southern Missouri. It was once prettier and quainter than its surrounding smaller towns with their flat, plain layouts and

23

unimaginative downtowns. Forrest City was an inviting stopover for motorists heading east because of its ivy-covered hills, good restaurants, peach tree groves and genuine community.

No outside door was ever locked in the home where I grew up. No screen door was ever latched, unless it was warped and threatened to let mosquitoes inside. When people knocked at the door, nobody asked, "Who is it?" We simply sang out, "Come in!" and looked up to see who had dropped by. Our home was open to anyone, anytime and for any reason.

On summer nights I would lie in bed, feeling the sweat of my body sticking me to the bottom sheet. Often it was so hot that I'd kick down the top sheet till it lay in a crumpled pile at the bottom of the bed. We would have suffocated if the windows remained shut, so every screen was kept patched to prevent the mosquitoes from carrying us away.

On one such night, as I lay there listening to the music of insects, waiting for the occasional breath of wind to glide over my perspiring body, something rather special happened. Suddenly, the sound of insects was accompanied by the soft musical sounds of a choir singing hymns. Many additional voices soon joined in.

The week before, I had observed workmen as they diligently labored in the July heat assembling the tent, complete with center poles, sawdust floor and a platform stage. The First Baptist Church had used the park since the 1930s for its annual summertime tent revival. The large cloth out front advertised, "Tent Revival Tonight!" I had no idea what a revival was.

Curiously and quite naturally, when I heard the singing, I slipped out of bed and out of my seersucker pajamas. I donned a t-shirt, shorts and sandals and followed the sounds out the front door into the sweltering night air. I stood on the curb peering into the big tent. I was seven or eight at the time. I think I told Grandma where I was going. She may have wondered what I was up to, but I had a lot of freedom growing up in a place like Forrest City, where folks were friendly and pretty much trusted each other. Grandma did not mind me going out to visit in our neighborhood. Like me, I do not think she knew what a tent revival was.

As I approached the tent, the "greeters" seemed somewhat surprised; nonetheless, they handed me a program and a small fan. Someone took me by the hand and led me slowly through the front entrance to a seat next to a kindly older couple. They were singing with considerable emotion while gazing upwards, presumably toward heaven. The usher winked as he seated me. The older gentleman smiled reassuringly, and he leaned over to share his hymnal with me. I felt strangely drawn by his kindness. I sang songs like "Rock of Ages", "Old Rugged Cross" and "Jesus Loves Me." I didn't know what they meant, and it sure was different from the singing I'd hear in the synagogue. I noticed the choir in the front rows and I liked watching them.

I could not repeat what the evangelist said that evening because I do not remember. It was the people who drew my interest. Many of them were going forward to be "saved." "Saved from what?" I wondered.

Whatever it was, those who had gone forward seemed relieved afterwards, as if some weighty burden had been lifted from them. Although it was difficult to make sense of it all, I drank in the spirit of joy that filled the tent.

I was welcomed again on the second night. I was perfectly comfortable; the event seemed as natural to me as Forrest City itself. I went straight to the front row, and they even let me sing in the choir.

By the third day, all I could think about all day was the preacher's invitation to come forward and receive Jesus Christ and be "saved." I had already decided that I would go forward that night. So when evening came and Grandma reminded me that my two favorite cousins from Chicago had called and would be in town soon, I startled her with my "salvation intentions." She had no idea what I was talking about so she let me have my way.

After bounding across the moonlit street I found "my" seat and waited to walk down front as others had done. Finally, when the pastor looked out over the crowded tent and invited the lost to repent and be saved through Jesus Christ, I walked down the aisle with a few grownups and stood in front of the elevated pulpit. I said a prayer asking God to forgive all my mistakes and wrongs. I left that night feeling elated.

Later, when Mom and Dad found out what I had been up to, they didn't know whether to be amused or upset. "Grandma, you shouldn't have let him go to the Gentiles' church service," Dad scolded.

"Nonsense," she replied. "He's a Jew and he'll always be a Jew. He knows he's different. He was just being neighborly."

For many years, the story of that evening was the source of a good family joke. Particularly amusing was the oft repeated, "Charles is in the Baptist choir."

Grandma was right. I did know I was different, perhaps more than she realized. There was no doubt in my mind that I was a Jew. I felt very Jewish and enjoyed it. Mom and Dad spoke Yiddish around the house when they didn't want us to understand, as did my grandparents. We had a typical Jewish home. But Forrest City, Arkansas was not a typical Jewish neighborhood. I felt very comfortable among Gentiles and particularly with the African-American culture. It may not be politically correct these days for "white people" (we Jews never considered ourselves exactly white) to employ people of color as drivers or housekeepers. But that was the way of life in the where and when of my childhood. And these folks were like family to me.

Forrest City was ground zero for the blues. I remember when Cross, my dad's driver, took his turns in the carpool that took a few of us to our Sunday School at the big Baron Hirsch synagogue in Memphis. Whenever Cross drove, I'd skip Sunday School to go riding around with him. We'd talk, and we'd listen to the radio. He'd always tune in those black blues stations to listen to John Lee Hooker, Bobby Bland, Nat King Cole and others. I really admired Cross. And I was fascinated by the music he'd play and the stories that went with it.

I found an honesty among the black community that seemed very real and very right to me. Obviously, I was not a part of that culture, but in some ways I related to it more than to my Jewish roots. It's not that I rejected my Jewishness. In a sense, I enjoyed the best of both worlds, but didn't feel completely a part of either.

Still, imagine what must have gone through the minds of the folks in that tent when they saw the little unattended grandson of the very Jewish Snyder family wander into the tent, lip-syncing along with the church choir and walking forward in response to the preacher's call to the lost! I cannot believe there was any cultural precedent for that in the 75-year history of Jewish settlement in Forrest City.

I'd left the tent that night excited about my experience and bubbling over with the news. I was not prepared for my mother's consternation. She is such a gentle woman, and this was one of the few times I remember her being really stern. She let me know that Jesus is not for the Jewish people.

I was disappointed and could not really reconcile what she was saying with my experience. It had felt right to go forward in that tent. I thought about what I had done for the next few days. I wasn't entirely convinced that it had been wrong. But before long, the experience faded, and I moved on to other things.

Considering the broader context of the rest of my story, it certainly was predictive of things to come. My life followed a strange, uncertain, circuitous and often quixotic course for the next thirty years.

CHAPTER SIX:

LIFE LESSONS

"I don't know why you won't send me a check, Jimmy. You know I love you more than your mother does!" Dad's tone was respectful but firm.

"Why, what do you mean?" the surprised young welding shop proprietor asked.

Dad finished his point: "You know she only carried you for nine months. I've been carrying you for a year and a half."

Jimmy's guffaws could be heard clear across the room. Two days later, Dad received a check for the balance of this slow-paying customer's account.

The little one-horse company that Grandpa Snyder started back in 1921 had grown into a large company with satellite operations that easily supported six families.

Dad and Uncle Reuben became 50/50 partners after Grandpa Snyder died. I remember the night Grandpa passed away. When he and I went for our nightly drive to get an ice cream cone at Ferguson's Drug Store, nothing seemed wrong. Later that night, I awoke to sounds of panicked desperation. Dad was rushing down the hallway past my bedroom door with Grandpa—who was gasping for breath—slung over his shoulder. He flopped Grandpa into the back seat of the car and raced two blocks to the Crawley-Cogburn clinic. Dr. Crawley met the car curbside. In his hand was a long hypodermic syringe filled with epinephrine, which he promptly thrust into Grandpa's chest—but Grandpa was already gone. That is how we lost the man who had been a father to me the first few years of my life.

In Jewish families, when a patriarch leaves a void, someone moves in to fill the vacancy—someone the other family members respect and trust. Even though my father was only the son-in-law and not the "heir apparent," in the Snyder clan, he was the only one prepared to fill the void. His track record of sharing his time, money and other personal resources with the family made him the top prospect. He also enjoyed offering his opinions in just about any situation. So when the "position" opened, so to speak (it was a matter of who the family naturally looked to, nothing official), Dad rose to the occasion, stabilizing the family and the family business.

That business, E. Snyder & Company, consisted of a large salvage yard with scrap iron, metals, pecans, hides, furs, cutting and welding supplies—and anything else that would sell. They bought and sold it all, including railroad paint by the barrel, unused WWII bombshell casings (farmers used them for culverts and irrigation systems), and animal bones that were used for jet fuel.

The war years were very good for the scrap or "junk" business, and many good businessmen made fortunes during and after the war. Scrap dealers bought up and sold many war salvage items, such as jeeps and half-track trucks, for large profits. Raw materials were so valuable to the war effort that scrap dealers were exempt from draft status. Dad did not have to go to war—he could have stayed home and profiteered from it as some have been accused of doing—yet he went and served his country because he felt it was right to do so.

After the war, Dad's incredible energy for new challenges erupted into bold and imaginative ideas. Foreseeing the post-war building boom, he convinced Uncle Reuben that a warehousing retail operation for new steel and pipe was their ticket to prosperity. And it was! By the mid-50s, daily truckloads of steel, pipe, tubing and wire were shipped from our warehouses in all directions throughout the tri-state area and beyond.

By the time that Uncle Reuben's sons (Martin, Richard and Conrad) and I started working for the company, it was doing so well that we did not have to work (although we found plenty to do). The business provided important opportunities to work alongside our dads.

It is good for a boy to labor alongside his father, watching him address problems, finish tasks, and even, on occasion to see him fail. That is how I learned about myself, and ultimately how I came to define myself. History confirms that no society can exist very long without that father-to-son transfer. Sadly, the father-son bond is missing all too often within today's society. I am thankful for the years I spent working alongside Dad, even if at the time it seemed monotonous and restrictive.

Dad's keen business instincts could identify merchandise that others would pass over as "un-sellable." He would buy it at a steal, then literally create a demand for it. For example, when a Missouri-Pacific freight train derailed just north of Cape Girardeau, Missouri, Dad flew up to take a look. He spotted the 2,000, 55-gallon drums of maroon, silver and white, industrial grade, outdoor paint strewn along the tracks. He bought them all for five dollars a drum and convinced the railroad to deliver them to his doorstep. He then "created" a market for the paint by explaining to farmers that it would prevent their plows and land levelers from rusting. And he convinced owners of cotton compress warehouses—huge storage sheds that were roughly the same shade of maroon before they faded in the delta sun— to take advantage of the bargain price. They bought the paint for a dollar a gallon, a profit of about 1000 percent, even after labor was included. Everybody won. That was Dad's way of doing business and the reason for his early success.

Countless episodes such as this caused the company to boom. It seemed like Dad and Uncle Reuben couldn't make a bad business decision. Dad handled the new steel and pipe division. Uncle Reuben skillfully managed the scrap and brokerage angle, making large profitable deals with customers and brokering merchandise for smaller dealers without actually having to handle the merchandise and pay out for labor.

It was an experience for my three cousins and me to watch our fathers meeting after-hours in the big private office they shared. Cigar smoke saturated the air. They spoke words *at* each other, but mostly they communicated through body language. You only knew a decision had been made and an agreement reached once they stood up, paced the floor and removed their hats to scratch their heads, all the while chewing on their cigar butts but neither one looking *en face* at the other one.

If they did not want us to know about something, they would begin speaking in Yiddish. There, I had an advantage over my older cousins because I had lived with my grandparents, who spoke a blend of English and Yiddish. It was fun to know what was going on, then to keep it to myself. I was so much younger that my cousins wouldn't have believed me even if I had told them what was going on!

Each of us boys learned how to buy pecans, grade metals, load and drive bob trucks and tractor-trailer rigs, maneuver forklifts, wait on customers, value merchandise, keep a day book and communicate with employees. We also learned to laugh a lot. Everybody had a wonderful sense of humor, beginning with Dad and Uncle Reuben who both had a knack for telling funny stories and cracking one-liners.

A customer once bitterly opined, "Heck, Reuben, a dollar ain't worth nothing anymore."

"It's not?" Uncle Reuben responded dryly. "Well, then, how about letting me take some off your hands for six bits (75 cents) each?"

The customer, expressionless, thought about it for a few moments, then burst out laughing.

That is how it was, all day, every day. Back then, everyone got along really well. Vacations were rare. Business doors stayed open, except for the occasional scorching Arkansas, July afternoon when we couldn't shed enough clothes to keep cool and our dads would "shut it down," load us all up and head straight for the old municipal swimming pool for a cold dip.

Once, after a paralyzing, statewide ice storm, no one opened their business except Dad. He'd found his old ice skates in the attic and skated downtown to the store through the main streets of Forrest City. I can still see him carving figure eights on Grant Street. As a boy growing up in Chicago, he had often skated with his friends on the frozen ponds at city parks. No one in our little community had ever witnessed ice skating, much less skating on the streets. Everyone was watching him with delight and respect. I was so proud that he was my dad!

By the mid-60s, all of us were making lots of money. We had more privilege and perks than almost anyone else we knew. We boys were presumptuous enough to believe that when the batons of leadership were eventually passed to us, we would excel even beyond where our fathers had prospered.

Over those years, Dad taught me far more than the value of a dollar. There is not sufficient space to relate the extent of his compassion and philanthropy, most of it done inconspicuously. When prison guards were regularly beating his brother, Dad fixed it. When another brother was going bankrupt and was about to be punished by the mob for non-payment of gambling debts, Dad intervened. When four nieces were in detention because their errant mother was in jail again, Dad stepped in. When a young friend of the family could not afford postgraduate educational expenses because his own family couldn't provide financial assistance, Dad was there. When a business customer or friend had personal financial difficulties and struggled with legal problems, Dad came to the rescue. Dad always "fixed it" because his character and conscience would have it no other way. His involvement in the lives of others was as predictable as sunrise.

In his prime, it seemed the whole world sought out my father. It seemed everyone benefited from his benevolence and generosity—from the hitchhiker on the highway, to those at the top, including congressional leaders, governors, doctors, judges, lawyers and businessmen. He quickly rose to leadership in any organization he chose to involve himself in because of his natural abilities and approachability. When the call to leadership came, he responded quickly and decisively. He presided over the local Lion's Club, the Masonic Lodge, the Crowley's Ridge Shrine Club, the Synagogue board, state and regional B'nai B'rith organizations, the Leo N. Levi Hospital for Arthritis, the Memphis Jewish Home for the Aged, the Crowley's Ridge Annual Horse Show and the Forrest City Airport Commission—just to name a few.

Dad held active positions with other philanthropic organizations, some of which were worldwide. Major decisions were envisioned and implemented in Dad's hotel suite; many deals were brokered in Dad's cigar smoke-filled parlor. He presided over a large contingent of people always waiting to be told what to do next or to invite him to their respective regions to give new life to a "stalled" agenda.

Dad's influence was everywhere. All across the country, folks were eager to do something to help Louis Barg. Once, in 1961, I was in Dallas, Texas, en route to a Razorback football game at Waco. A friend and I had difficulty making our airline connection out of Dallas. When we were unable to find a hotel room in the city, I called Dad, who loved to be able to use his connections to help his son. Dad called Stanley Kaufman, an attorney friend who lived in Dallas. Stanley called a friend who owned a burlesque lounge a few blocks from the phone booth where I had placed the call. A few minutes later, Stanley phoned me in the booth and told me to go a few blocks south to the "Theatre Lounge" and ask for Jack, the owner, who would "take good care" of us.

When we arrived, the doorman was expecting us. Without hesitation, he ushered us to the best table in the house where we were treated to free steak dinners and drinks. During the show, after our stomachs were filled with prime Texas beef, Jack showed up and told us that he had arranged for us to stay in a nearby hotel room. His bouncer would drive us there whenever we were ready to leave. It was first class all the way.

As we left, Jack patted me on the back and said, "I don't know you son, but any friend of Stanley Kaufman's is a friend of mine." "Jack" turned out to be Jack Ruby, the former Chicago mobster who shot Lee Harvey Oswald. Two years later, I saw him again, but this time it was live on television, when he gained worldwide notoriety by ambushing Oswald. Stanley Kaufman was Ruby's attorney of record during the arraignment and trial.

In 1963, on the occasion of the fiftieth anniversary of the Anti-Defamation League of B'nai B'rith, Dad and I flew to Washington, D.C., for an event called "Dinner With the President." President John F. Kennedy was the guest speaker. If a bomb had exploded at the Rock Creek Park Hotel that night, most of the leadership of the United States government would have perished. Everyone was there—vice-president Lyndon Johnson, Chief Justice Earl Warren, the Pentagon's top brass, and many more of Washington's elite.

It was a special night. It was also the night that I realized more about the world in which Dad lived and thrived. He seemed to know everyone and was on a first name basis with most. He appeared so at ease in such company, so handsome in his tuxedo. He didn't need a "cocktail" as a prop for conversation, just enough room to wave his cigar around when he wanted to emphasize a point.

Dad was not only well known for his generosity and social skills, but he was also one of the bravest men I knew. During the violent era of "Deep South" hate crime, the Ku Klux Klan flaunted their vicious, anti-Jewish sentiment. On occasion, captured Klan members became witnesses for the state and turned against their fellow Klan buddies in order to lessen their own sentences. Some of them had been involved in synagogue vandalism and plots to kill Jews in Mississippi, Alabama, Georgia and elsewhere throughout the South. Dad helped organize a network of Jewish businessmen in border states who would provide these Klansmen with short-term "jobs" until it was time for them to give their testimonies in court. Then the FBI would arrive to pick them up and take them to a local jurisdiction for a speedy trial, after which they would be hastily transported to another state to await the next phase of the prosecutorial proceedings.

Of course, the lives of these former Klansmen were in danger, but so were the lives of anyone willing to offer them safe harbor. Some of these men— murderers, arsonists, terrorists, kidnappers and assorted felons—worked beside me day-to-day loading trucks and handling the forklift. Some even spent a night or two in our home from time to time. Dad never flinched when the call came to help one of these men who was willing to testify against the Klan. When lesser men might become fainthearted and retreat, Dad proved his beliefs by his willingness to put his resources and his personal safety on the line.

One summer evening during the 1970s, Dad learned that Robert Shelton, then Grand Wizard of the nationwide Klan movement, was coming to Forrest City to exploit the racial unrest dividing the community. After work, Dad drove out to the tent meeting and took a seat near the front row. The tent soon filled to capacity with spectators, all supportive of Klan dogma. Dad recognized many men and women whom he had known for years. Some were his customers. Shelton spent most of the evening unleashing scathing diatribes against black people. Then, in the last thirty minutes, he blamed all of society's problems on "the worldwide Jewish conspiracy."

After the meeting, as the crowd was leaving, a man Dad had known for years moved up close to him and confided somewhat apologetically, "We don't blame you Louis. You're not like the rest of them."

Without hesitation, Dad answered, "I just came out to hear what he had to say. But Billy, I'm a Jew through and through. If anyone hates my people, he hates me as well!"

Dad was no more afraid to confront that circle of danger than he was to confront any other issue that required real men to step forward. It has been said that, "Tyranny reigns when good men say nothing." Dad was a good man with something to say. I learned from his humor, foresight, compassion and bravery every day of my young life.

CHAPTER SEVEN:

TODAY A MAN, TOMORROW, A SEVENTH GRADER

"What's a *bar mitzvah*?" It never occurred to me that my seventh grade pal, Alva Archer would have no idea what I was talking about, no clue regarding my anticipated ascent to Jewish manhood. Scarcely concealing my pride I answered, "That's when I become a man."

Despite my pride in "becoming a man," I awaited the day with more anxious resignation than excitement. I was going to have to stand up and sing in Hebrew in front of more people than I'd ever stood before in my life.

My dad never had a bar mitzvah because his parents had spent the money for his older brother, Jack's bar mitzvah, and there was none left for Dad—not for the Hebrew lessons nor the accompanying celebration that would have followed the ceremony. Jack—who ended up in plenty of trouble—received the Jewish education while my dad—who stayed out of trouble and exemplified many qualities lauded by his religion—did without that all-important milestone.

That missing milestone, along with the fact that he never made it past the eighth grade, deeply affected Dad. He was quite open about the latter, particularly as he ascended the leadership ladder of B'nai B'rith. "I didn't even finish school," he'd say, with something approaching pride—and he had reason to boast. With his limited education, he still possessed the skills to move ahead of people who had all sorts of degrees to become the international vice president of B'nai B'rith. Dad knew a lot, more than most, when it came to figuring things out. But he was always painfully aware that he was not an educated man.

As such, Dad's knowledge of Hebrew was limited. Yet every day after dinner he'd sit down and teach me what he did know—the alphabet and the sounds each letter makes. He took me as far as he could, then made arrangements for me to learn from the rabbi.

Every Wednesday I boarded a Trailways bus to Memphis, then I caught the Jackson Avenue city bus out to the Baron Hirsch synagogue. If the lesson concluded early, I would stroll along the downtown streets of old Memphis. I loved Beale Street with its pawn shops, fruit stands and Lansky Brothers Clothiers—where I later learned Elvis Presley usually shopped. Elvis just may have been shopping for that famous flashy wardrobe of his while I stood outside the store, my nose pressed against the window.

So I studied and prepared for the big day. And though I was fearful about being in front of all those people, I was far more afraid of backing out. It's not that I was afraid of God. By the time I was twelve, doubt regarding God's existence had taken root. I considered myself an agnostic, meaning I didn't believe in God or act as though he existed, but I left the door slightly ajar in case I was wrong. My fear was not of God, but of embarrassing my family, of embarrassing myself, of being different from the other Jewish boys if I didn't go through with it.

Jewish boys traditionally become bar mitzvah (literally "sons of the covenant") at age 13. Girls who undergo the ceremony (as has become more common today) often do so at age 12. Becoming bar mitzvah requires the boy or girl to accept responsibility for his or her own sins, for keeping the traditions of Judaism, and for faithfully passing the torch to the next generation.

Customarily, the bar mitzvah *bochar* (boy) leads the *Shabbat* (Sabbath) service, which is held on Friday evenings and Saturday mornings. He chants the Hebrew prayers before the Scripture readings and chants the Hebrew Scripture readings themselves as well. Then he gives a speech to the entire congregation. It usually expounds a portion of the Scripture he has read, as well as honoring his parents, relatives, and of course, the rabbi.

Somewhere in the speech, there is also a call to remember both his Judaism and the nation of Israel, which are henceforth supposed to be his *raisons d'etre* in Jewish life.

By the time I turned thirteen, apart from familial expectations, my bar mitzvah seemed more like an excuse for a good party than anything else. Typically there would be feasting, dancing and an open bar. Whereas I was nervous about chanting in Hebrew and giving a speech in front of everyone, I looked forward to the music.

I always had a lot of rhythm, so I enjoyed dancing at family functions—bar mitzvahs weddings, things like that. My dad took me everywhere with him, especially to the B'nai B'rith functions. Everybody was always dancing. When I was only nine or ten years old, older girls and women taught me how to do dances that nobody in Forrest City knew how to do, from cha-cha to mambo to waltz. My dad was a great dancer too, and he taught me some steps as well. Music helped me develop confidence and a way of relating to others. I enjoyed it, but with the exception of the blues, it was more of a tool than a passion.

I knew that the dinner and dance following my bar mitzvah would be something special. Bar mitzvahs were (and I suppose still are) frequently viewed as a measure of a family's economic prosperity and community influence. Thus, many families even competed to see who could have the largest or most creative event. Bar mitzvahs have been known to translocate to Europe, Israel and points all over the globe solely for the novelty of it.

By the time I turned thirteen in 1955, Dad was serving notice to the local Jewish community that he had arrived. There were a lot of Jewish families in the Mississippi Delta. The big cities, like Memphis, were more likely to have a large concentration of Jewish people, but we were also scattered throughout the surrounding areas. B'nai B'rith was the common thread that tied in the Jews from small towns like Forrest City. When we small-town folk came to a big city, we tended to put on an even bigger deal than the people in Memphis because we, in a sense, had more to prove. These small-town folk worked hard and when we came to the big city, we made sure the red carpet was ready.

My dad planned a glitzy blowout. He rented two floors of the Hotel King Cotton in Memphis and invited everybody he knew: our extended family down to the last fifth cousin, the Jewish community at large, business associates, a large Gentile contingent of friends and anyone he could think of who had never seen a bar mitzvah. Everybody received a written invitation *and* a phone call; almost everybody came.

The Hotel King Cotton was a grand old hotel by the river in downtown Memphis, just off Front Street. The hotel had window air conditioning, which was somewhat of a luxury in those days. It boasted a grand ballroom. The tables were covered with classy linens and real silver. Memphis had two or three exceptional hotels and the King Cotton was definitely one of them. Dad rented a room for just about any out of town guest who needed a place to stay. He picked up the tab for everything.

My bar mitzvah was like a carnival. Dad's side of the family was pretty rough. They drank and smoked and often got into fights. My mom's side was far more genteel. I remember fearing what Dad's family might do in front of my friends.

My dad's best friend was Danny Trabish, a Chicago boy he'd grown up with. Danny had a night club across the river in West Memphis. In fact, just a few months before my bar mitzvah, Danny kicked a young man out of his club—a guy he'd hired to sing there—because he didn't like his friends. That was Elvis Presley. Most of the adults who came to my bar mitzvah ended up in Danny's club at some point—drinking and dancing.

Some of my dad's family had brought what I knew as "bad movies." I remember some of the men kind of clustering together to watch, but not my dad. I was relieved that he was not like them. I was proud of Dad, but I didn't want my friends in Memphis to know about his family. Many of our guests were community friends, bankers and businessmen from Forrest City. I kept hoping we could get through the event without them seeing that some of my relatives were not quite respectable.

Things went fairly well, and the speech went particularly well. In fact, my dad enjoyed it so much during the ceremony that he asked if I'd do it again at the dance. And I told him, "Yeah, I'd like to." I remember that everybody gathered around to listen that night. I'd seen my father speak so I knew how to take my time and make eye contact. I began, "Worthy rabbis, beloved parents, relatives and friends . . ." I remember thinking, "This is kind of like Dad." I really wanted very much to be like him.

For all of the pomp and circumstance of my bar mitzvah, I do not remember much mention of God. In retrospect, nothing from the preparation or actual event guided me to believe in God; neither did it even tweak my interest enough to ponder his existence. It did confirm my identity within an ancient and respected heritage, affirming me as "somebody" in connection with my people. Some believe this is the primary function of religion today.

It is interesting to watch the strange interplay between the need for individuality and the need for conformity or identification with a particular religious viewpoint. To some degree, these needs seem to conflict with one another. It can get very confusing.

My bar mitzvah was a corporate as well as an individual experience. In a sense, it was a fulfillment of my father's dream. But I also remember people saying, "You're going to be a man." Dad especially. He was so proud. My bar mitzvah is actually one of the few times I remember him patting me on the back, telling me what a good job I'd done—no suggestions, no critique, no stories of his own. I remember basking in the glow of Dad's approval the day after the bar mitzvah, and wondering how my life would change.

I was a bit shocked in the days and weeks that followed that I didn't feel any different. I remember being a little disappointed that I didn't feel more manly. Still, I'd been through something and somehow people were calling me a man regardless of how I felt or didn't feel. This was a very different experience than that of my Gentile friends.

Growing up in a predominantly Gentile community, most of my best friends *were* Gentiles. We were the "Baby Boomers," so from kindergarten through college, many new facilities opened just in time for us. We were a close-knit group. I never felt like the token Jew; I fit in quite easily.

In high school, I participated in some sports and dating, and I went to parties with everyone else. We had a couple of high school fraternities in Forrest City, which at one time, did not allow Jews. I was popular enough to receive bids from both the fraternities.

I pledged the Delta Sigma fraternity and they had some pretty big guys. A lot of them went on to play college football, and some even went beyond that. We met Monday night and as pledges, we took quite a bit of abuse. Part of our hazing consisted of gathering in a little room where we had to strip down to a pair of underwear and an athletic supporter. We all waited with some amount of dread until they finished their business and called us into the meeting.

When we came into the room they had various games, probably the least painful of which was known as cuckoo. One pledge was sent under a table, another was posted on top with a wadded up newspaper. When the guys hollered cuckoo, the one under the table had to stick out his head and the guy on top whacked him with the newspaper.

The one that scared us the most was when they took one guy and paraded him before the president of the fraternity. He'd ask the guy questions, then finally say, "Okay, we're going to leave you alone. You just sit down. If you feel like singing, just stand up and sing." And since we didn't know what was to follow, we each thought, "You must be crazy if you think I'd sing in front of these guys." So we'd sit down in our underwear and then a couple of minutes later we'd hear this peculiar whirring sound and we'd discover that the chair had wires hooked up to a hand cranked generator. And they'd shock us, so we'd jump up and sing "God Bless America" until they told us to shut up.

The hazing wouldn't be complete without "High Life," a substance used for Tennessee Walking Horses to make them hold their tails high. We'd have to drop our britches and they'd apply some High Life and make us run. Words can't describe how painful that was—the only relief was to sit on a cold car bumper. I don't know why we allowed them to torture us like that in ninth and tenth grade, but we did. Maybe that was the Gentile rite of passage—part of their idea of becoming a man, I don't know. I only knew that I wasn't going to be the one to chicken out.

My Jewish friends in Memphis wanted to know all about the fraternity. They were a bit incredulous about the hazing, and in a way seemed to admire me for being able to take it. They were also curious about the other activities I did with my friends in Forrest City—water skiing, fishing and such. Likewise, my friends in Forrest City were curious about what I did with my Jewish buddies in Memphis. Each seemed interested in how "the other half" lived. I was comfortable in both worlds, but never felt completely a part of either.

Sometimes my Forrest City friends even invited me to visit their churches. I think I visited every type of church within the city limits. I found nothing particularly interesting or compelling about any of those experiences—nothing like my boyhood "revival" experience. To me, it was all just social. No friend ever told me about Jesus; maybe they figured that if I visited their church something might sink in. It never did.

I never saw Christianity as a better way of life or a better set of beliefs— it was just what well behaved non-Jews were supposed to believe, at least in the South. In many ways Christianity seemed as traditional as Judaism, except that we Jews have much more history. And I reasoned, was not their Messiah himself a Jew? He didn't go to church, he went to a synagogue like I did. Maybe he even had a bar mitzvah!

CHAPTER EIGHT:

JUNCTURES

"Here comes another drunk redneck who wants to hear Johnny Be Good *for the umpteenth time."* That's what I thought as I bent down to take what I assumed was a request. Instead, still smiling, the guy reached up and gave my microphone a shove—right into my teeth. Before he could do anything more than cut my upper lip, the bouncer had "escorted" him from the premises.

So how did a nice Jewish boy end up playing guitar and singing lead in a rock n' roll band?

It started a month before my high school graduation. I'd driven up to the University of Arkansas campus in Fayetteville in my cousin Richard's brand new, convertible Pontiac Bonneville, a sleek "hummer" of a machine. It was spring, 1960 and we'd come for a music festival. My friends and I stepped into Rockwood Club in Fayetteville and were met with raucous, intoxicated greetings.

Everyone was carrying beer mugs, two at a time, as if there was a drought in the land. Ivy League dress and manner were in. If you wore anything other than a button-down Gant shirt with a full pleat down the back, khaki pants, blue blazer and penny loafers, you were considered to be from the *nawth* (north). The look and feel and taste of life miles away from home were pure adventure . . . *and the music!*

Ronnie Hawkins and the Hawks were playing that night. Ronnie owned the Rockwood Club and played there a few months each year when he was not in Ontario or Quebec, Canada, but I had not heard his band live before.

45

Newly famous for a nationally renowned hit record, they were heroes among the college crowd.

Most bands playing around the area were local guys who practiced in someone's garage when they were not out driving tractors or working on cars. Ronnie and the Hawks were unlike anything we had ever seen or heard. They were tremendous musicians, each demonstrating an impressive virtuosity on his respective instrument. Plus, they sang and harmonized with inventiveness, precision and an easy, sophisticated style. The combination was electrifying!

A few years later, the band, "minus" Ronnie became better known as Bob Dylan's band or simply "The Band." A few albums and a grand slam appearance at Woodstock later, critics began speaking of them as the band that best defined the period of music when rock and folk music married. Eventually, The Band was inducted into the Rock and Roll Hall of Fame. Their lead guitarist, Robbie Robertson, became one of the better known musicians of the era.* Even today, folks around Arkansas remember the first time they heard the Hawks' kind of music. They were ahead of their time.

Obviously I had no idea of where they were heading when I first heard Ronnie Hawkins and the Hawks, but I knew that I was in the presence of great talent. So did everyone else in the room. We all stopped and stared when Robbie Robertson stepped forward for a guitar solo. Flipping the toggle switch on his old, fret board worn, maple-necked Fender Telecaster, he undulated the instrument's volume with his right pinky finger, coordinating that with a deft, string-stretching left hand. His fingers stretched the strings to the upper limits of the fret board. The music mesmerized us, filled our senses, captivated us. It was both exhilarating and scary.

I'd grown up drinking in the sounds of the delta blues that filled our airwaves every Saturday afternoon via the KFFA King Biscuit Flour Hour. The show brought us live performances by Sonny Boy Williamson, Howlin Wolf, B.B. King, Little Milton, Lightnin' Slim Harpo, Muddy Waters and

---

* Eventually, when The Band broke up, Robbie became good friends with Martin Scorcese. He did the music for *Raging Bull*, and played in a movie called *Carnie*. One of Scorcese's films, *The Last Waltz*, chronicles the life and times of The Band.

whoever else happened to be visiting "back home" from Chicago's Southside developing blues scene—which consisted mostly of vagabond, black southerners.

These artists were as yet "undiscovered" by white commercial markets. We happened to know about them because they played down the road from us. So when we heard the all-white Ronnie Hawkins band playing this same great music, playing it well and even adding some interesting new twists, we found them amazing—even irresistible. I never knew white guys could sound like that.

I rushed out to Beale Street and bought a Fender Telecaster. Before long, my college days were over—at least for a while. The Hawks usually came down from Toronto for about six weeks at a time to play all the little joints around Arkansas and at the University of Arkansas. I started following them wherever they played. Eventually, we became good friends, and I began traveling with them.

Robbie taught me a lot about the guitar, as did Rick Danko, the bass player, who was an excellent lead-guitar man as well. Levon Helm was my closest friend in the group. He originally hails from Turkey Trot, not far from Forrest City, so we related to each other in a special "Delta" kind of way.

Before long, I was playing lead guitar for a band called "The Mystics." I was never great, but Robbie taught me how to cover my weaknesses—and more importantly, how to connect with the audience.

"It's all about showmanship. It's not about how fast you play, but how you 'phrase' the notes," he used to tell me.

Soon I was imitating Robbie's style and that of other great guitar players who were kind enough to teach me. I practiced constantly, composing music in my mind while driving down the road or lying in bed at night. Often, as I drifted off to sleep I'd think of a musical expression, get out of bed, pick up my guitar and play through the night until I was satisfied that I had a piece just right.

"The Mystics" started off playing anywhere we could draw a crowd. That meant small town jubilees, taverns, fairs, picnics, class reunions, local talent and TV shows and smelly roadside juke joints, where the cigar box housing the night's "take" was often mysteriously "light" when it came time to settle up at the end of the evening. But a gig was a gig as long as it paid travel expenses, including the obligatory 3:00 a.m. steak platter at the local truck stop where we would stop to top off the evening with friends and sometimes family after the show.

Sometimes we played between fistfights. Other times, we were the object of a scuffle. One night we played a club out in the middle of a cotton field near Osceola, appropriately named "The Rebel Club." That's where a young man with a duck-tailed hairdo and a cigarette in his mouth sauntered up to the stage—seemingly to give us a request. Without warning, he shoved the microphone into my teeth while I was singing a ballad.

My lip was bleeding, but not enough to stop the show. The club bouncer beat on this particular "rebel" all the way to the door before lifting him off his feet and throwing him into the parking lot. I managed to finish the ballad without further interruption. Our drummer later suggested dryly, "He (my attacker) must not have been in the mood for a ballad."

We never knew what set the guy off. We had found, on occasion, that if certain girls paid too much attention to us, we were likely to become objects of their boyfriends' wrath.

Eventually, several members of "The Mystics" were drafted into the Vietnam War. Our remaining members joined with a few other musicians and called ourselves "The Unit." We practiced more seriously and were treated accordingly. We played classier engagements, like the Peabody Hotel and the Top of the 100 Club in Memphis, as well as numerous college campuses.

When we began playing some of the Memphis gigs, Dad would sometimes bring a whole entourage to see us. Now Dad was a big fan of swing music, and especially Bing Crosby. As such he didn't particularly like our music. After all, it was rock 'n' roll; it was never intended for his generation. Nevertheless, whenever I did anything well enough to gain recognition, he was pleased for me, and proud.

Our popularity grew and our sound got "tighter." Sometimes we played Conway Twitty's Moon Lake Resort down in Mississippi. Conway's mother, Mrs. Jenkins, would always bring out Conway's Fender guitar (a gift from the Fender Corporation when he received his first gold record). Every time we played her club, she would approach me as we were setting up and ask me to play that guitar for her. Knowing how much she treasured it, I felt honored.

As with any good local band that has its eye on the "Big Time," we were optimistic and determined to do whatever it took to make it. And a common

myth among musicians was that it took drugs to reach "the next level."
We do what we have to do to serve our chosen interests. As the Dylan
song proclaims, *You Gotta Serve Somebody*. Like everyone else, I found
myself inclined to pay homage, give tribute, to something or someone.
Consciously or not, I guess I knew there was something greater "out there"
in the universe. I didn't understand my own need to worship, which made
me that much less likely to find the one worthy of that worship. Like most
people, I settled for icons. What an appropriate name for the little figures
on our computer screens! Icons—gods!

It is easy to pursue the "gods" of art, entertainment, possessions,
intellectualism, self-awareness, self-promotion, self-fulfillment, meditation,
monasticism, asceticism, philosophy—even religion. I'm sure I thought
myself too sophisticated to consider music, art, job, spouse or children
"idols" (substitutes for God), but what else are they if one exalts them as
the source of meaning, fulfillment and purpose?

Music became my icon. Unlike God, however, music could not love me,
protect me or, in the deeper sense, provide for me. It did not feel or care
about my loneliness. Like so many others, I counted on my music to do
more for me than it ever could. That is always risky.

Danger lurks in an unseen world around us—the supernatural realm.
Many of us long to "take a peek" into that world, although some do not admit
it. I know that this hidden world exists because I've "been there." Whereas
I thought I was mastering music, the truth was actually the reverse. I'm not
saying that music is evil. It is a powerful gift, but it can be abused and
manipulated for selfish pleasure or as an object of false worship.

It is tempting to use music as an opiate; to surrender and give one's self to
it. It is no surprise that many people equate the "next level" of musicianship
with alcohol and drugs. Who needs God when we can create our own
"supernatural experience" most anytime we wish, even if it is temporary?

I was never much of a drinker and wasn't attracted to drugs for the sake of
getting high or being "cool." The idea—much less the feeling—of losing
control was unappealing at best. Yet when I saw friends like Robbie and
Levon using pot, I wondered. They explained that all the musicians in Canada
used it. If they felt it made them better musicians, I wasn't going to dismiss it.

Eventually, Robbie and Levon invited me to smoke some pot with them.
My wife-to-be and my sister were with me that night to hear us play at

Gabby's 11/70 club. Robbie and the guys wanted me to ride back with them and meet the girls at the restaurant where we had planned a late supper. They offered me a joint on the way and by the time we met up at the restaurant in Lonoke, I was high for the first time.

The other guys acted cool, almost like they were into another level of awareness. They laughed about things that other people didn't understand. They were friendly with the others, yet winking at each other in that "insider" kind of way people do when the rest in their company aren't entirely "in the know." I felt a part of that, and it felt good.

In the car on the way home I told my girlfriend that I'd smoked some pot. We'd been dating for about a year, and she let me know she didn't think it was a good idea. I don't believe I promised never to do it again, nor did I make specific plans to get high in the future. In fact, I smoked periodically but didn't make a habit of it.

One time when Robbie and the guys came to Arkansas, his amplifier broke. I let him borrow mine. When I went to use it after he returned it, I found a huge joint taped to the toggle switch underneath it. I remember thinking it was pretty good stuff.

I have watched good musicians who used drugs become bad musicians—even though the drugs gave them the illusion that their music was extraordinary. I have also seen average musicians play far beyond their natural talents when they use mind-altering drugs. The latter seemed to be my experience, at least at first. Musically, I went places that I had never been before—the same place that turned the simple, early Beatles music of 1964 (music that almost any southern band could imitate), into intoxicatingly seductive music filled with hidden meanings.

The drugs sometimes made me feel that time had slowed to half speed or slower. Sometimes I felt the moments go by so slowly that it seemed as if seasons could change between the notes. It gave the illusion of limitless time to be inventive and to create rhythm expressions between notes, bars and stanzas.

One night I showed up for practice high and watched myself playing notes and phrases that I had never practiced or even heard before. Afterward, everybody, including the groupies who followed the band, expressed amazement and wanted to know whose style I had been copying. They wanted to listen to me all night; I wanted to listen to myself! Every bone and sinew within me wanted to follow that "light," no matter where it should lead, no matter the cost.

I have heard this experience described as "spiritual," "soulful" and "righteous," I believe there was a spiritual influence controlling me that night, pushing me past my own abilities, enabling me to create more exciting music than I was capable of on my own. I absolutely believe it was a power beyond the chemistry of the drugs. But it wasn't a benevolent power.

My first inkling that I was entering a hazard zone was in 1965, at the Forest Hotel in New York City on 49th and Broadway. I was in the company of some of the great musicians of that time. We were in a large, seventh floor suite where we had been practicing and exploring new sounds and rhythms for days. Everyone was stoned on some exotic form of weed, which might well have been "dusted" with a hallucinogen.

We'd been playing a couple of days, and they kept rolling the joints. My heroes were showing me how to play all sorts of different rhythms, and I didn't want the music or the smoking to end.

In fact, when it came time to take a shower, I would periodically poke my head out of the shower to take another hit. After the shower, I dressed—we were getting ready to go to Harlem that night—and went back out to the living room. There was a knock on the door. And suddenly, I was out of my mind with terror.

I went for the door, but Robbie or Levon moved in front of me to answer it. Two guys I didn't recognize stood there. One of them (later I found out it was John Sebastian) extended his hand to greet me. I grabbed his hand and yanked him through the threshold so I could get past him, and I was out the door like a shot. Levon and some others chased me because they realized that something was very wrong.

They chased me down the stairs. I ran down the corridor testing all the doorknobs. I was overcome with the delusion that "they" were going to kill us. Paranoia. Finally one old man opened his door, and I pushed past him, picked up the phone and called the police. When the police came, there was a big commotion. Levon came down and said, "Everything is going to be okay, this is our friend," and he kind of talked me down with the policeman standing right there. Levon probably kept me out of jail that night since I had no idea I was behaving like a maniac. Eventually, I calmed down and went back upstairs with them.

That was the first time (but not the last) I realized that what I was doing could be dangerous to me. Each time I got the picture, it frightened me. I came to suspect there was something evil behind it all. It was a vague suspicion, yet I could not shake it.

It was as though a war was going on within me. The pull of the music/celebrity lifestyle was much stronger than a twenty-two year old like me could resist. God knew that, and I believe he protected me. He would always either frustrate my plans to move around the country and live with The Band (who were like gods to me), or he revealed glimpses of the darker depths of the drug-dependent life to which I was being drawn.

The lure of the inexplicable talent I sometimes seemed to possess when I was high just could not compete with the inexplicable terror I also sometimes experienced—or with the fact that I was beginning to see lives ruined by drugs, and I didn't want mine to be one of them. I realized I was doing the same things as many whom I'd watched come to ruin. That frightened me—and unlike the inexplicable terror, it was a good fear.

It became clear to me that the cost of following my friends through the next door was too high for me.

Too many who went through that door were destroyed. Too many great musicians died and many who remain are struggling to survive. Where did all the peace, love and harmony go? Did not the sixties promise it all to us forever?

Definite junctures in life determine our eternal destinies. We don't always know those junctures when we see them, and it's easy to follow promises that eventually lead to nowhere. What may seem like a well timed circumstance, or a wave of intuition, or even a feeling of foreboding, just might be a touch from a merciful God, waiting patiently by the juncture, calling us to something bigger and better—something we don't yet understand how to want for ourselves.

CHAPTER NINE:

LINDA

"The 1953 Little Miss Forrest City beauty pageant winners are . . . Linda and Belinda Coley!"

Enthusiastic applause filled the Forrest City High school auditorium as twin seven-year-olds stepped forward to receive their crowns from a smiling John Henley. Henley owned the local florist shop and enjoyed his perennial role as host and emcee of the Little Miss Forrest City beauty pageant.

Pageants and parades were a big part of social life in southern small town America. I loved going to all such happenings with my parents. As Jews, we were somewhat of a community unto ourselves, yet we were also very much a part of the larger community and supported every major event that the town sponsored.

Linda Coley, co-winner of that year's pageant, was three years younger than me. If I'd noticed her before the pageant, I don't remember, and we scarcely noticed each other after. But a decade later, when my sister Barbara pulled up to a popular drive-in, in my new convertible with Linda Coley in the passenger seat, I noticed. If Linda was cute at seven, she was stunning at seventeen. I can still see her smile. Pretending I wanted to chat with my sister, I casually wandered over and said "hi" to them both.

A few months later, I asked Linda out on a double date. We went to a Memphis movie house, and afterward, dinner at the Polynesian Restaurant. I knew from the start that I would love her; that she was the one I wanted to marry. The fact that we came from very different worlds was of no consequence to me.

As a child, Linda had attended a Presbyterian church, mostly under compulsion by her dad, though he was not religious. In Forrest City, "good people" simply went to church on Sunday. Folks who had no church affiliation were not necessarily "bad people," they simply lacked evidence of being "good people." Everyone knew "who wenteth" and who didn't. Of course, there were those who "wenteth" too much, which was almost as bad—and some considered it worse. The "right" amount of church conferred a degree of respectability upon "good people" without particularly threatening anyone. It imbued the word "Christian" with a cultural, rather than spiritual, meaning.

These were the social mores that defined decency down in Dixie, and that is the mold from which Linda emerged. She did, however, have one deeply spiritual person in her life—her grandmother. Grandma Coley was a loving role model who prayed regularly for the granddaughter that she— a midwife in the small farming community of Pumpkin Bend—helped bring into this world.

Grandma Coley raised five sons and no daughters. She was industrious, gentle, kind and generous. She spent her entire life in service to others. Anyone who met Grandma Coley experienced her "light" shining brightly. Her example inspired Linda to want to be a wife, mother and moral person.

Now my mother and father had always talked to me about the importance of marrying a Jewish woman. They lived with the same concern that most first and second generation Ashkenazim (Eastern European Jews) in small towns experience—that their children might marry Gentiles and within a couple of generations, the family would no longer be Jewish. To some extent, I was sensitive to my parents concerns. In fact I had been dating a Jewish girl from Memphis when I saw Linda at that drive-in.

Jean was smart, pretty and came from a very good Jewish family in east Memphis. She was everything that Jewish parents would want in a daughter-in-law. But Jean and I never had the connection, the chemistry that Linda and I had from the very start. Jean was quite independent, which was admirable, but it didn't draw me to her. She didn't need me the way Linda did—in a way that I needed and wanted. Linda had a way of looking at me like no one else. And whatever I may have thought before I saw that look, once we connected, it mattered very little to me whether or not she was Jewish.

While Linda was not outwardly independent like Jean, she knew what she wanted and had plenty of determination. Her mother was not a nurturer and her dad was often passive about family issues. Linda saw a dynamic of warmth and interdependence in Jewish families, and she was determined to have that.

The first six months of our relationship were electrifying. We spent all of our time together. We'd go hear Ronnie Hawkins and his band at the dances. I'd take her out to eat in Memphis (the "big city") and to the movies. We were so excited about sharing how we felt and what we wanted that I'm not sure either of us ever proposed marriage to the other. We began talking about it early on, just assuming that it would happen.

But of course marriage does not "just happen." And I was a selfish young man. I loved Linda, and I loved sharing my heart with her. But once I knew she loved me too, I took her for granted—a lot. I wanted to do and to have everything. And my parents, hoping that I'd come to my senses and marry a Jewish girl, did not encourage me to commit myself in a way that Linda deserved.

As for Linda's parents, I'd known them from way back. They used to run the local drive-in movie theater. They liked me well enough, knew and respected our family and so forth. Linda's dad was probably somewhat worried—not because I was Jewish, but because I had a reputation for being a little wild.

Some of Linda's friends cautioned her not to get involved with me. Her best friend's mother was a sponsor for the cheerleading squad (of which Linda was a member). She would tell Linda, "Now you know he's Jewish, and you really shouldn't marry a Jewish person—they're *different*." Linda recognized that the lady meant well and even appreciated her concern, but never heeded the advice. That isn't to say that we didn't experience the usual challenges in our relationship.

Linda went off to college—a small Baptist school where her grandmother had been a trustee. I had a brief stint at Memphis State, but returned home to pursue music and work for a while, in the family business. Linda and I saw each other on the weekends. She'd get on a bus and come to Memphis or we'd meet in Forrest City.

I missed Linda terribly, and eventually she began to wonder if I was ever going to ask my parents for their blessings on our plans. I kept hoping they would warm up to the idea, but they never did—and I kept putting off the inevitable confrontation.

Linda had continued as a cheerleader in college and the captain of the basketball team was quite taken with her. Her sister was dating the co-captain, so it seemed easy and natural for Don and Linda to spend time together too. Exasperated by my indecisiveness, she began to accept his invitations. The love of my life, dating the captain of the basketball team—this did not bode well.

By all accounts, Don was a nice guy, the kind I imagined parents would want their daughter to marry. He was big, athletic and straight as an arrow. I was worried about Don. I tried to be nonchalant about my feelings when Linda came home for Thanksgiving, but it didn't work very well. When she came home for Christmas vacation, I urged her to stay, promising that we would court and marry. She did not return to college, but took a job in Forrest City.

Linda and I talked about marriage for two years, and still I got nowhere with my parents. They liked Linda, they'd known her since she was a little girl, but my mother—one of the most gentle and least judgmental people I've ever known—was absolutely appalled at the thought of my marrying a Gentile.

When I insisted that I wanted to marry Linda, she and my dad seemed to relent. "We'll go talk to the rabbi about it and we'll take Linda," they promised—but they never followed through. Finally, I got tired of waiting. Linda and I decided we'd elope. We got the rings, the cake and the dress. The big day arrived, and I put on my suit and walked out the door. I was headed toward the car where Linda, Bill (my best friend at the time) and his wife, Joanna, were waiting. Then I heard my father's voice. "Charles?"

I turned to face him. He was calm, respectful and firm as he asked, "Son, can I talk to you a minute?" It was a Saturday and one of the few times he was at home. I had not discussed my plans with him or my mother, but he knew what I was about to do. "Look," he said, "if you'll put this off, we'll go talk to the rabbi and do it right."

I believed him. And because I believed him and did not want to disappoint him, I said, "Okay." It broke Linda's heart, but she did not argue. Days later, when I said to my parents, "Okay, let's go talk to the rabbi," they did not want to talk about it.

I moved out of the house, into an apartment in a complex where Linda was also renting. One night, I went by her apartment after baseball practice (I was coaching Little League) because I thought I was going to surprise her and we'd have dinner together. I knocked on the door. She came out awfully quick and stood with her back against the door. She was wearing something I'd bought her in San Antonio; a bright two piece outfit I'd found while attending a B'nai B'rith convention. She seemed distracted. I knew she was not alone.

I must have sounded like the stereotype of the silver screen boyfriend as I demanded, "Who's in there?" She said, "Nobody," but being the truthful person she is, she was utterly unconvincing. I moved to open the door, but she blocked me. I grabbed her hand and demanded once again, "Who's in there," and this time she told me. "Don. Don is in there."

I was so hurt, so angry—yet I couldn't blame her. I'd allowed my parents to stall our plans and had not made any further moves toward marriage. I was spending a great deal of my time learning guitar, traveling with the band, pursuing musical ambitions. She'd given up school for me, and was not seeing a great deal of return on her investment. When Don called, she'd had no reason to turn him away. She'd cooked dinner for him in the outfit I'd bought her and there was nothing I could do.

We talked later that night. She told me she wasn't sure, she was confused—the usual things people say when they're trying to break off a relationship. Which is precisely what she did.

For the next three months, I could not sleep more than two or three hours a night. I couldn't eat. I was sick. Every country song I heard about lost love seemed to have been written for me. Worst of all, I figured that probably the best man had won. Finally, I started dating another girl to try to get on with my life.

One night at about eleven o'clock I looked out my window, and there was Linda, walking her poodle past my door. She looked like she wanted me to notice her. And then she walked by again. I went out and just looked at her. I don't think we said a word.

Soon after, my band played a dance and she showed up with another guy—not Don, whom I grudgingly admired, but someone who I felt obviously didn't deserve her. And she sat at the front table under my nose.

Later that night, I knocked at her door. I said, "Look, if you have to leave me, at least go with somebody who's going to treat you right. This guy's a jerk. The other guy—I don't know him—but I know he has to be a good Christian guy." I didn't really know what a Christian was, but I remember calling Don a good Christian guy—because of its social and cultural connotation.

That's when Linda looked at me in that way she has, and she said, "I'm not interested in either one of them." We got back together, and I'd never had a happier moment.

It had been about a year since my parents withheld their blessing. I went and told my dad, "We're going to get married." He asked me when and I told him it would be within two or three weeks. He said, "I really wish you'd wait and talk to the rabbi." I said, "No Dad, we've been through that. It's been four years. Linda and I are going to Colorado, and we're going to get married."

We planned a date. We rented a house in Forrest City and painted it, with help from Linda's dad. My dad was getting ready to go out of town and I informed him, "We're leaving this weekend to get married." He replied, "Well, don't leave until I come back from Little Rock." He was going to see his sister Rose who'd been ill. I said, "Dad, we're leaving first thing Saturday morning and that's it."

That Friday night, we were out late at a gig but when we finished, Linda's dad came over and helped me pack up the car. We were up and out before the sun the next morning, and we headed off to Colorado in a Jaguar XKE, a 1966, 12-cylinder convertible. I had just purchased it, used and cheap, which is exactly how it performed. We had all of three hundred dollars left to our name.

By about six o'clock in the morning we were coming through DeValls Bluff, which is halfway between Forrest City and Little Rock. Amazingly, we passed my dad going the opposite way on the road. Ours were the only two cars on the highway. Dad was apparently making tracks to get back and talk to me. He slammed on his brakes, bringing the car to a shrieking halt and sat there, honking the horn. I accelerated and gave a backward wave as Linda and I kept on going.

Dad just wanted what was best for me. But I'd finally come to realize that he didn't always recognize the best when he saw it. His love for me was wise, but not all-knowing. It played out in mostly truthful ways, but was not above some degree of manipulation or trickery. All well-intentioned—but flawed. I was not so philosophical at the time. I was angry.

The anger was short-lived as Linda and I arrived in Denver, hoping to have something of a Jewish wedding. We looked in the phone book, located the nearest Reform temple, drove there and somehow convinced the rabbi to meet with us for a pre-nuptial interview. He listened to our story, but would not marry us. We left Denver for Greeley, where a municipal judge united us in a civil ceremony at the courthouse. By coincidence, he happened to be Jewish, so we felt that that just might add a small measure of Jewishness to our union.

A cold reception awaited us back in Forrest City. My family, particularly my mother, did not speak to us for nearly three months. Nevertheless, when our band was playing at a New Year's Eve party at the Hotel Peabody in Memphis, the whole *mishpochah* (family) came. At the stroke of midnight, Linda jumped up on the bandstand to wish me a hearty, "Happy New Year." Suddenly, Dad appeared beside Linda, hugging her and crying. He motioned for Mom, and helped her up onto the stage, where she too, embraced Linda. And suddenly, everyone was hugging and crying, including the band and the crowd! Linda Coley was lovingly enfolded into the Barg family once and for all.

Linda did not want our future family to be divided on matters of religion. She was intrigued with the Jewish way of life, which is known for its family-oriented, traditional style. Her own parents had eventually divorced once their three daughters were out of high school, and she was searching for a different model. Therefore, Linda decided that she would become a Jew.

Contemporary Judaism is not a religion that encourages conversion. Linda pursued the Orthodox rabbi for several months, but he followed tradition by alternately ignoring and discouraging her. Linda was unfazed and continued to pursue her goal for several months.

Eventually, she was able to convince the rabbi of her sincerity, and with his help, my bride converted to Judaism. From that point on, Linda had an advocate in that rabbi. He kept a special place in his heart for Linda throughout his tenure at the synagogue.

Soon after Linda's conversion, we were married again. This time the rabbi united us to the Torah in a Jewish ceremony attended by family and old friends. My parents were elated. They not only had a daughter-in-law they loved, but after they had lost all hope, they found their son was married to a nice Jewish girl after all.

At the time of her conversion, Linda was three months pregnant with our first child. As my anticipation of fatherhood grew, my interest in the band waned. The rock music scene lost much of its appeal as I watched it become a wasteland for so many damaged, disenfranchised people. Many were drugged-out, with nothing to show for the years they had spent in almost total devotion to the music. Nothing, that is, but a seemingly ceaseless tendency to rehash stories of past good times that probably weren't as good as they remembered.

One night in Helena, at a joint called "The Showbar," I surveyed the scene through my new, "pre-paternal" eyes. The music was loud, the lights were flashing, and the crowd was looped and lusty. The rawness of that scene suddenly struck me as inappropriate for a married man with a baby daughter on the way. It suddenly occurred to me, "If my father was living like this, I would be ashamed." That's all it took. I knew it was time to put away childish things and be a *mensch*. I quit the band that night and never looked back.

CHAPTER TEN:

HIS SON THE DOCTOR

I opened the door just in time to hear Martin say, "Louis, you S.O.B." I was enraged at my cousin for speaking that way to my father. Without stopping to think, I confronted him. And everything changed.

***

I'd reported for work at my father's company the very first Monday morning after I left the band. Linda's smile let me know that she was proud of me and feeling more secure in light of my renewed enthusiasm for conventional employment.

Being the youngest in a family business is difficult. It was particularly so for me because it had been years since I had shown an interest in the company. My cousins *had* shown an interest, had fully invested themselves and their expectations in their careers. Suddenly, there I was, as if from nowhere, all primed and ready to make my mark on the family business. My cousins didn't know what to make of me in this new role. They liked me well enough, but did not respect me as a colleague. Up till that point, I hadn't given them cause to.

Now that I was a "family man," I injected myself into Dad's area of the business with all the determination of a young man who knows he has a lot of ground to make up. I was determined to rise early, sell merchandise, load three trucks at a time, complete the paperwork, check the billing, assume nothing, question everything, attend company meetings, go to bed late—and so I did, without hesitation, for a year and a half.

However, eighteen months into my new life I realized that no amount of hard work could change the fact that "business" between us boys was simply not working out.

Dad had accomplished what he did for the business because the time was right and he was the man for the job. No one else had the ability to step up to the plate and get it done. That was not the case for the next generation. Dad and Reuben were still getting the job done and did not have the slightest intention of pulling back. They didn't really need me— plus three hungry young men stood in front of me, leaving me as the lowest man on the "food chain."

It didn't help that Dad's portion of the company would eventually go to me, while my older cousins, by now junior partners in the firm, would split their father's portion three ways. I believe that fact contributed in large part to the disintegration of close family friendships into open, undisguised enmity.

I'd tried to tell my father that it wasn't working out for me to stay in the family business. "Dad," I told him, "it is obvious to me that as the youngest member of this company in general, and as your only son in particular, my cousins will never accept me as a lifetime business partner."

I tried to tell him that his dream of two families living and interacting together as one in this incredibly successful business was, in fact, only a dream. I knew he had witnessed an increasing volatility in our daily interactions. Yet he would not listen to my assessment.

"Charles, you're always running scared," he'd say. That was how he'd dismiss everything I wanted to say on the matter. Then he went on to tell me, "They are family and family is supposed to stick by each other and get along." Ultimately, he'd tell me, all you really have is your family. The word "family" was probably the most often repeated word in his vocabulary.

Even the most uninvolved hired hands in the company knew that there was great tension among us. All of us cousins were working side by side in the office, barely acknowledging each other's existence. If a customer called for one of us, whoever answered the phone would say, "He's not in."

It was then up to the customer to decide whether to call back or go with the person answering the phone. There was a hostile competition, even though none of our individual incomes were dependent on the amount of sales we generated.

The only one who didn't seem to see the heated rivalry was Dad. He was the unifier, the peacemaker, the counselor. He used to tell me, "You're always imagining that your uncle and cousins don't like you. It's like when I was district president of B'nai B'rith and Sammy Grossfeld would call me up . . ." He'd launch into a personal anecdote that drifted far away from the point. And I could tell that he really didn't understand.

A chasm had destroyed the unity Dad had sought to establish. We'd all been so close growing up. Now we were chafing at that closeness. Resentments were ready to boil over into open warfare.

That was the climate when I walked into the office one day and heard my oldest cousin, Martin, speaking to my dad with the utmost disrespect.

Martin was the oldest of the Snyder cousins and in "the good old days," he was my hero. He was about nine years older than me, so he and Dad were close before I was even born. Martin was smart, athletic and handsome. I always looked up to him. He and my father remained close as I was growing up. Dad introduced Martin to flying and even allowed Martin to fly his airplane. He gave Martin lots of encouragement and treated him, in many ways, as a son. However, as Martin got older he began to act resentfully toward Dad.

Martin and the "middle" brother, Richard, made plenty of money for their families. They had ample time off, the company paid for their automobiles, many personal bills such as home utilities, even their housekeepers—all in addition to the generous salaries they were making. When Martin and Richard became partners, my dad and my Uncle Rueben had each given up 20 percent of their 50/50 partnership for the two of them.

I had my own conflicts with my dad, but it made me angry to see anyone show disrespect for him—particularly these boys, whom he had treated so generously.

Apparently Martin had been trying to get more interest from my father, who was unrelenting. He told Martin, "No, we've got the two younger boys coming in (meaning myself and Conrad, Martin's youngest brother). Reuben and I are going to give each of them ten percent of the business."

I came in during that conversation, just in time to hear Martin say, "Louis, you S.O.B."

My dad was a strong man, and few men would knowingly provoke him. Everybody knew, however, that he would never raise a hand to a family member. He was willing to take the insult. I, on the other hand, was not.

Normally, I would avoid trying to resolve a situation in a physical manner. But when I heard him speak to my father thus, a surge of adrenaline energized me. I charged up to Martin, made an equally crude remark as I suggested the two of us go outside. We went out to a scale that was used for weighing trucks, a big open area. I got right up in his face and let him know I was ready to fight.

Months before, Martin and I had had a fistfight and wrestling match. It had started as "horseplay" that quickly became serious. I remember feeling vaguely surprised that I was stronger than him. I'd been working pretty hard in several aspects of the company, which included lifting and loading steel.

The confidence I'd gained from overpowering him that day, added to the strength my rage had pumped into my fists made me more formidable than I would have guessed. Several people jumped in and broke up the fight before it came to blows. But before they did, I thought I saw fear on Martin's face—and I was glad of it.

Somebody had grabbed hold of me and somebody had grabbed hold of Martin and he was furious. "You're fired!" he snarled, and I spat back, "You impotent little #@&*!, you don't have the authority to fire me."

We called a company meeting. Martin's dad was there and so was mine. They agreed that because my dad was a partner, Martin couldn't fire me. To my amazement, Martin's behavior toward my father was not even an issue.

Dad truly did not seem to care about what Martin had said. His response to my anger was, "It's okay, you gotta put it past you, they're family, you can't go against family, you can't raise your hand to your family." My dad simply could not admit that there was an unbreachable rift in our family.

I said, "Dad, how can you accept that your nephew—to whom you gave part of your business, for whom, in many ways you were like a father— would insult you in front of the whole office, and in front of me, your son? And you're not mad?" I was angry that he wasn't angry. My father had a certain standard, a certain grace, a certain unconditional love concerning family that was way beyond me.

I kept my job, but I lost any hope that things would work out between my cousins and me. I wasn't afraid of conflict but I did not want to spend my life in a place where I would never be accepted, but always resented. I realized, with some regret, that I was not going to be there for the rest of my life. Regret because I had always wanted to follow in my dad's footsteps, always wanted to grow up to be like him, always wanted to please him. But I did not fit into his world, and I did not want to spend my life as a misfit.

My decision to leave the company produced a feeling of euphoria—for about one day. I had no college education (I'd abandoned school for music), was untrained for anything other than my father's business, and had a family to provide for. I hadn't yet told my dad that I was planning to leave. I knew I needed to stay put until I was certain of the next step, until I had figured out what to do.

One of the first questions people ask one another when they meet is, "What do you do?" For so many of us, self-esteem comes from having a satisfying response to the "wha-da-ya-do" question. We fear having to admit that we do nothing; that we have not found a niche in the world (though once we have found it there is even greater fear of losing it). We are used to thinking that what we do defines who we are and what we are all about. Without that something special to do, we may not be able to understand why we "exist." Others may not value us.

I'd been working hard six or seven days a week and was starting to get my own customers. My dad was proud of me. What would he think of me when I left? What would I think of myself? These questions led to weeks of doubt and second-guessing.

One evening, while visiting a longtime friend in Memphis—an internal medicine physician—I mentioned my recent decision to leave the company. I confided that at age 26, my future seemed frightfully uncertain.

"Well, why don't you consider medicine?" he said straight-faced.

I waited for the punch line. Taking into account my age and total lack of preparation for anything requiring an academic background, he might just as well have asked me to reverse the north-to-south flow of the Mississippi River.

"Kenneth," I said, "I have no background in the field of science. It would be impossible."

Ignoring my response, he smiled gently, gazed philosophically toward the ceiling for a moment, took a long pull on his pipe and added, "I believe that anyone with average intelligence and considerable perseverance can do it. In fact, I'm certain of it!" He didn't try to be overly persuasive; he just let me know that becoming a physician was attainable if I didn't mind a lot of work. That was news to me.

In fact, following their high school graduations, my cousins Martin and Richard had left Forrest City to go to Louisiana State University, to become doctors in accordance with their mama's wishes. Their mama was named Develling, but I called her Aunt D. I recall her as a rather mean woman who didn't seem to like anybody except her own children. She certainly didn't like me. One time she told me I looked like a donkey. That can make a deep impression on a six-year-old psyche!

Aunt D used to tell my mother, "My sons aren't going to be junk dealers like their grandpa. *My* sons are going to be doctors." The first two boys went off to fulfill her dreams. However, they didn't make the grades so they came home and went into the company business. Why should I expect it to be any different for me?

Yet here was my friend Kenneth, telling me that without a doubt, I could do what my cousins had failed to do. Cousins who, in my estimation, had caused me to leave the family business. We'd certainly become aware of our differences in the last eighteen months. Maybe college would be different for me. Maybe I could succeed—and wouldn't it be sweetly ironic?

Driving home that evening, Linda and I didn't speak much. Just before we crossed the St. Francis River bridge near "Cabin in the Cotton," Linda asked me, "Why the silence?"

I hadn't even realized that I was waiting for her to ask. My heart opened and possibly for the first time, I poured out many thoughts and feelings I had never before fully sorted out for myself. I shared my life's ambitions with her: what I believed and who I wanted to be.

Until that evening, my goals had been rather narrow and fragmented; life had always just "worked out" for me. No one on my father's side of the family had ever even graduated high school or college, much less attained a postgraduate level degree. I thought about my grandfathers' pioneer spirits and realized, "Here is a pioneer opportunity for me."

"Linda, I've decided to become a doctor," I concluded the speech with a decisive nod.

She answered softly, "I know. That's what I thought you would do when I overheard you and Kenneth talking." Moving even closer to me and looking up into my face, she smiled her big smile and confidently exclaimed, "Hello, Dr. Barg!"

That's all it took. Through Linda's unconditional love, I discovered that I could make something of my life. She was so confident of my outcome that I started to believe it myself!

I still had a family to feed, so I needed to plan and be patient. A couple of months after the altercation with Martin I had a heart to heart talk with my dad. I told him, "Dad, I always felt like eventually I would come into the family business and spend the rest of my life here working with you. But I've come to realize that it's really not the place for me. I don't think there'll ever be peace at the company again with me there, and I don't think I'll ever feel secure about my life trying to fit in when I belong somewhere else. I want to be a doctor.

"Would you give me one year to see if I can make the grades? I'll move to Memphis and go to night school. I'll commute back here and continue to work with you for a year during the day. (Memphis was about 48 miles away.) At the end of a year, if I've made good grades at night school, will you let me go to college full time? I'm already a few years behind, and I've got to feed my family. If I do well in school, will you pay for me to become a doctor?"

He tried for a while to talk me out of it. He told me I could work things out with my cousins if only I'd try. He said something to the effect of, "You know a man works hard so that his family can have something, and I've done that. I've always dreamed that my son and I would be here and work together in the business. That's what a man lives for."

I held my ground. I told him, "Dad, I really do realize that, but look, Dad, my cousins don't care much for me, and it's going to get worse. I'm not willing to spend my life trying to please them."

When my father realized that I no longer saw the family business as an option, he let me know he would support my decision. It wasn't a hearty, "Okay boy, go get 'em." I understood he was disappointed, just as I had been, that I would not be following in his footsteps. I also knew that once he agreed to help me, I could count on my father to see me through. He was always a man of his word.

Linda and I moved to Memphis with our daughter, Alison. I grabbed as much of an academic load as I could, 18 hours. I'd leave Memphis at six in the morning, work all day, copy my notes at night, go to class, recopy my notes, then dictate them into a recorder so I could listen to them on my drive to Forrest City the next day. And I made straight A's.

When I made the honor roll, they printed it in the Forrest City newspaper. My dad realized this was not going to be such a bad deal after all. He got vicarious satisfaction from my academic success. One morning he called me into his office and said, "Son, I'm proud of you. Go, do well and you can count on my support until you finish." With that, he reached into his desk drawer, produced his checkbook, handed it to me and granted me instant access to his personal financial resources. My grades and the recognition that came with them had taken the sting out of my decision to leave the business.

I began attending classes during the day. As a student volunteer in the registrar's office, I was able to get around the 18 hour maximum work load. I sometimes took as many as 22 hours, and managed to finish 132 hours in just slightly less than three years. I graduated with honors, a Bachelor of Science degree and an invitation to join the freshman class at the University of Arkansas School of Medicine for the 1972 school year.

Medical school was fun. From a curriculum standpoint, I did not find it as difficult as Kenneth had suggested, although it was the busiest four years I'd ever experienced. By graduation day in 1976, Linda and I had four children: our oldest daughter Alison, as well as Sam, Margot and Joshua, who were born during my college and medical school years.

Linda single-handedly kept our little family together during those years. At the same time, she made time for me, fastidiously and courageously staying the course through it all. Usually she still managed to be smiling when I returned home at the end of the day.

I should add that medical school did not encourage personal, family life and as a result, by graduation time, nearly thirty percent of our class was divorced or separated; many other marriages did not survive the postgraduate years. Many medical students are tempted to treat problems as things that patients have—but not us. As though doctors are above such things. Obviously we are not.

My postgraduate training included quite a bit of moonlighting around the state in various mid-to-large-sized hospital emergency departments. I found I enjoyed taking care of a range of problems from diabetes to high blood pressure, to eczema and even cancer. I wanted to help people who were depressed, had bipolar disorders and so forth. I liked having an actual part in seeing patients live longer, fuller lives.

Several guys I'd gone to school with were starting to go into practice. Among them was Mike Hendren, who one day said to me, "Why don't you become a family physician?" At the time, I'd been moonlighting quite a bit at the emergency room of the Baptist Medical Center, so I was right there on the campus. (In the South, frequently the biggest hospital in town is the Baptist Hospital. I never thought much of it from a religious standpoint.)

I happened to know there was one office space left on the campus. I walked in one day (after being up all night in the emergency room) and said, "I'd like to buy this office." I believe I was speaking to the president of the corporation of the building. He said, "Well, we're pretty old over here. We'll rent it to you, but we're not selling any of this space." I proceeded to pull one of the biggest bluffs in my life. Everybody knew that Barg Steel Company was my family. So I went over to the Baptist administration and made a great deal of noise about buying the adjacent property. I was in no position to do so, but they did not know that, and were afraid I was going to have a whole new building under construction. The next morning they called and said, "If you want to buy the office, it's yours."

So I got by with that one. I opened a solo practice as a family physician on the campus of the Baptist Medical Center. After twenty-three years, I continue to enjoy a full and satisfying practice. I've doctored everyone from the average man or woman on the street to some hospital health care administrators, to a few of our state governors. Forrest City being the small town that it is, has given me more than my share of "local boy makes good" recognition. This was a source of great joy to my father, and perhaps for a while, a source of irritation for Aunt D and a couple of her boys.

Eventually, I came to get on quite well with my cousins Richard and Conrad and their sister Marlene (with whom I never had any "family business" contention). Unfortunately, Martin had a falling out with the others and we don't see much of him. Regarding my medical career,

Marlene once wryly remarked, "You know, Charles, you ought to give Martin a birthday present, because if it weren't for him, you'd never be a doctor."

I suppose to some extent, she was right.

CHAPTER ELEVEN:

ROBBED BY ANGER

"Son," Dad told me, "don't ever retire. If you do, you're just another old man on a park bench. Nobody cares what you think." It was true that Dad had lost much of his influence, but it was never true that nobody cared what he thought.

When I left the company, Dad went through a long period of depression. My life had departed from his agenda. He always wanted the best for me, but it had never occurred to him that the best was something beyond his control, something that would not be his to give.

During this time, Dad also learned that he had contracted insulin-dependent diabetes. For the first time in his life, his sleep became interrupted. He lost his appetite and consequently, quite a bit of weight.

The next few years marked the beginning of Dad's decline. Unexpected struggles and disappointments took their toll. Even Dad's unique ability to forge compromise in the midst of adversity deteriorated into conflict with his business partners. People who once needed his wisdom no longer sought out his opinion; when they did, it was often a guise to ask him for favors, either financial or via access to his sphere of influence.

In 1977, Uncle Reuben died suddenly from a ruptured, aortic aneurysm. None of us realized how much Dad had sought Uncle Reuben's approval. While the effective, professional relationship that had worked splendidly for so many years had ceased by the time Uncle Reuben died, he and Dad still shared the same office building, even the same private office space. They had operated so successfully together and had survived many fires together, unscathed. Dad took Uncle Reuben's death hard. He lost about thirty pounds and a distinctive hollowness overtook his facial features.

It was only then that I realized that, in some ways, Uncle Reuben had been a father figure to Dad. I believe that Dad had always held onto the hope that Uncle Reuben needed him as well, that he valued their friendship beyond their business partnership.

No matter how depressed Dad became, he welcomed anyone who came to his door to ask for his assistance or opinion on any matter. This was his instant "poultice" for depression, even in later years when he was very sick.

Yet Dad couldn't stop ruminating about old, unfinished issues. He and Uncle Reuben's survivors never did agree on the final details of equitably dividing their common holdings—those details remained unresolved throughout Dad's lifetime.

Seeking to fill a void, Dad formed L. Barg & Company. He threw himself more passionately than ever into his work and philanthropies. He set up a home office cluttered with memorabilia commemorating past successes. He became co-owner of more businesses and assumed additional responsibility for other peoples' welfare and happiness. He hired unemployed relatives, many of whom were too old to work and just needed a place to draw a check. They appeared to listen attentively to his instruction, agreeing when he repeated, time and time again, his philosophy of business and life in general. However, they did little work.

Dad therefore did the work for everyone; he supported the whole flawed operation, laboring day and night with renewed determination. He tried to delegate decision-making responsibilities to his employees, yet everyone knew that no matter how they chose to handle a matter, Dad would later "suggest" how it could have been handled more efficiently and profitably.

He was patient and paternal in his unceasing criticism, but no matter how nicely it is served, a steady diet of criticism eventually deflates morale. When morale is low, apathy follows. Dad could not understand that others also needed to be "right" from time to time. I suppose he could not help feeling that he knew best, and perhaps he did. But he didn't seem to know that when someone's effort is good, and the results are good, it can sometimes be more productive to recognize what is good than to point out what might have been better. Dad *always* pointed out how it could have been better. An unqualified affirmation is probably the one thing in his life that he was unable to give. Aside from my bar mitzvah, I don't recall hearing him give an unequivocal word of praise. He just didn't know how.

This was true both in business and personal interactions and caused quite a bit of alienation in later years. Dad always needed to show a more correct way of thinking or feeling.

When Dad suffered a series of health setbacks in the 90s—including a heart attack and stroke—the straw house he had constructed collapsed. Slow paying customers, hearing of his misfortune, stopped paying. Some even ordered more materials for which they had no intention of ever paying. Employees became discouraged and made no effort to hide their lack of motivation. Everything unraveled.

Dad came home from the hospital, assessed the situation and closed the company. He sold everything and spent every dollar to pay off his bills. A lawyer friend advised him to hold back something for himself, told him that he deserved it after all his years of hard work. After all, the lawyer reasoned, his larger creditors would never take action against him at his age. Dad thanked the lawyer for his concern, but firmly told him, "I can't do that. What would my family think? A man has his reputation or he has nothing. At the end of life, that's all we really leave behind."

Once he retired, Dad's days were unfulfilling and his nights restless. That is why he warned me to never retire. He hated the feeling that people no longer cared what he thought. Nevertheless, people did care.

Most mornings I could find him at his preferred breakfast eatery, advising total strangers on any subject from fatherhood to personal business matters. Strangers admired and appreciated him, even when his body wasted away and his once proud stature and gait gave way to a wooden, shuffling footstep combined with partial blindness and trembling hands that spilled coffee as the cup approached his mouth. Each day he'd creep his car down along the busy boulevard to the little restaurant. He so needed to encounter somebody interested in what he had to say. If the place happened to be empty, then a waitress would do just fine.

Sometimes I would stand silently in the entryway to that restaurant, just watching him interact with people. I remembered the old days when I would listen with the same rapt attention, so proud that the wisest man in the world was my father!

Dad still had lots of genuine wisdom to offer at no cost. People loved him. And Dad loved finding solutions to help meet their needs and expectations. Many mornings I would arrive at my office to find someone waiting at the front door with the familiar story: "Your Dad and I have breakfast together a lot. He told me to come by to see you about my medical problem, and that you would take good care of me."

Many folks appreciated my father for his generosity and genuine interest in their lives. Everybody loved Dad, but most of us closest to him found it increasingly difficult to hear our ideas, thoughts and feelings continuously improved upon. Dad seemed unwilling or unable to listen to anyone else's point of view without somehow discounting it. This trait surfaced as he aged and was quite dominant in his later years.

In a typical scenario, I would explain to Dad how I perceived a certain matter. He would nod, appearing to listen. Then, he would begin a litany of remembrance, recalling minute details about past glories in business, the Marine Corps, B'nai B'rith or various family intrigues. I had already heard these stories numerous times and found it difficult to see their bearing on whatever topic I was trying to discuss. Eventually, Dad finished revisiting his past and came back to the present—to correct whatever I was trying to express, to tell me what I really felt or really wanted to say. Amazingly, he would rephrase the gist of my point in his own words, presenting it as the more accurate assessment. I was left feeling that he had managed both to discount my thoughts and take credit for them at the same time!

Perhaps those frustrating conversations actually did have a point of precision that could have added to my understanding—I don't know. It could be that I missed something good because of my ire at continually being told "how I really felt" and "what I really meant."

It hurt that Dad would continually criticize my perceptions; that whenever I tried to share my life experiences with him, he explained them away. He wasn't mean-spirited about it. He outlined very patiently why his was the correct and logical assessment. Our conversations were like a contest and often left me feeling drained, defeated and somehow trivialized.

At times, I didn't even want to open a conversation with my father unless I absolutely needed insight that only he could provide. I sometimes avoided interaction rather than dealing with the frustration of being continually corrected or having to listen to lengthy discourses on topics in which I had demonstrated no interest.

I wasn't the only one who had difficulty handling my father's seeming need to demonstrate his superior understanding of everything. I saw similar interactions with other people, sensed their dismay and felt embarrassed as they too, began to "shut down." My embarrassment was mixed with anger at those who shut Dad out. Even though I had similar feelings, I couldn't bear to watch people resent or disrespect Dad. I loved him and was angry with anyone, including myself, who failed to appreciate him.

And as I consider my dad with all his foibles, I realize that whatever disappointment or anger I may have had is mild compared to what so many other sons and daughters have experienced.

The world is filled with people who have not known a father's attention, protection or instruction. Some families have lost their dads to injury and illness. Others have watched helplessly while their fathers suddenly and unexpectedly packed their bags to leave forever. Too many children live in homes with uncaring, abusive fathers, or "replacement dads." Even worse, too many fathers simply ignore and/or resent a child's existence. This seems to be more often the case with sons, whom fathers may subconsciously see as a threat.

As a physician, I daily encounter emotional wounds that result from selfish men who someday, whether or not they care to accept it, must give an account for their actions before a holy God who sees all things. The most common response to those wounds is anger. Anger is probably the most common reaction to pain, though many of us prefer to call it something else.

Anger is a powerful destructive force we all face. And because most of us don't like to think of ourselves as angry people, the anger can go unaddressed for years. Others can usually feel our anger whether or not we admit it. As a result, we have a hard time understanding why people around us are "so oversensitive" or "become upset so easily."

Anger is a hunger for control that controls us. Without it, we tend to feel helpless to handle painful realities, or even painful illusions. Unnoticed and unchecked, anger robs us. Angry people give up more freedom than they know, remaining largely unaware of just how much their anger dictates their choices. And when those choices have destructive consequences, the person who does not deal with his anger will blame those consequences on others, perpetuating the cycle.

Of course there is a time and a place to be angry about the wrongs and injustices in the world. But too many of us waste our anger nursing our wounds. That's the kind of anger that controls and destroys.

That was true of me. Like many other people, I masked my anger—even from myself. There are different ways to do this; mine was through activity and accomplishment. I channeled the heat of my anger into energy, convincing myself that I was just highly motivated. Like many other people, I selected euphemisms, softer words, in expressing my anger. I was frustrated, hurt, disappointed, fatigued or detached.

Now I must be honest. I will not call my anger toward my own father anything other than what it was. It was the anger of feeling that my every thought and feeling was discounted by the person whom I most wanted to think highly of me; the anger of a son who's lost hope that his father will affirm him in the way he so desperately needs and wants. It was the anger of seeing him have his own need for affirmation met through near strangers rather than having real interactions with me. It was the anger of watching the strong hero who was able to handle everyone's problems grow weak. It was the anger of a son who feels that his own anger has marked him as ungrateful and unworthy of the father he still loves. All those things made me angry, but I could not admit it.

My father didn't lose control, so neither would I. Losing control is a sign of weakness. My father and I both feared losing control, particularly when we became angry. That fear of being exposed as an angry person is powerful. I wanted to appear cool and calm under pressure. I could not lose control, because others would lose confidence in me and that would ruin all that I had labored to construct. Or so I felt for many years.

But just like anger, fear must be masked. It is a sign of weakness. In fact, fear is the "backside" of anger; it is anger turned inward. Thus, fear affects people in the same way as anger.

I would eventually reach a point of being able to admit my weaknesses, including my anger. And eventually, that ability would enable me to help others do the same.

Anger can and often does surface as physical symptoms, and I have seen this firsthand as a physician. For example, a patient may complain of chest pain, insomnia, impotence, migraines, spastic bowel disorder, arthralgia, myalgia, neuralgia, lethargy and the like. Of course some patients truly suffer from organic, physically-based illnesses, but many others accrue these symptoms and syndromes as outward results of internalized anger. This is much more common than most realize, although science doesn't readily admit it. "Science" after all, is just a collection of human beings seeking to base all their conclusions on empirical evidence; nevertheless bound by their own preconceptions and biases. In addition, many scientists have their own unresolved anger to "mask" through activity and accomplishments. Scientists are not always as objective as they/we may like to think. Like everyone else, each has his or her own filters.

Angry people are often wounded people, desperately seeking self-esteem and, in many cases, using success as a measuring stick by which to compare themselves with everybody else. In order to fill shallow lives, wounded people often pursue such personal passions as business growth, worldly camaraderie and the worship of expensive toys and avocations. Even the most astute people are often willing to set aside most anything that seems to imperil their devotion to their own selfish choices.

Angry, selfish people have difficulty finding time for authentic, loving friendships or for rest and reflection. They *know* others, yet they themselves are *known* by none. That's because deep down inside *there is little or nothing to know*. Anger is a kind of bloatedness of the heart and soul. It expands, appears large and substantive, but houses an abysmal hollow. It crowds out the things worth having and knowing; it steals life away from us. Worse, it is passed on to successive generations, leaving damaged lives in its path. Often, we don't see our anger for what it is until we see peace, joy, vitality and lasting satisfaction in someone else's life and realize it has been missing from our own. And that is what happened to me.

My grandfathers, Sam Barg (left) and Israel Snyder (right).

Dad and Mom picnic in Forrest City 1941

Me and Mom 1946

Dad as a Marine 1944

A week in the life of Dad 1959

Louis Barg To Address McGehee B'Nai B'Rith

Louis Barg of Forrest City, will be the principal speaker at McGehee on December 15 at 3 p.m. at the 120th anniversary celebration of the founding of B'nai B'rith by the B'nai B'rith Dave Meyer Lodge No. 1084, according to an announcement of Max Zeno, president.

Louis Barg

Barg is the immediate past President of District Grand Lodge No. 7, B'nai B'rith and is currently serving as a member of the National Membership Cabinet.

In Forrest City, Barg has served as Chairman of the fol...

Dad (right) in Washington at an Anti-Defamation League meeting 1962

Dad as a
Vice President of
B'nai B'rith 1965

"The Mystics" performing in our
Beale Street outfits. We were the
opening band for the famous Charlie
Rich at the County Fair 1965
I'm on the far right.

Dad in Israel on a B'nai B'rith trip inspecting a
battle zone after the 1973 war

Dedicating the Sam Barg Hillel house
Fayetteville, Arkansas (Dad is standing
behind his two grandsons on the left) 1982

Dad meeting Jimmy Carter 1979

Linda (left) and her twin sister
Belinda win the Little Miss Forrest
City beauty pageant 1953

Our "second" wedding following
Linda's conversion to Judaism 1968

My son Sam and I fishing the Bow River in
Calgary, Alberta 2001

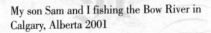

My brother, Mark 1989

Linda and me 2001

CHAPTER TWELVE

"I AM NOT A SINNER!"

"I'm trying to build a medical practice. Get mad if you want to, Linda, but I'll just have to go to Pinnacle Mountain with you and the children another time." My wife's look of disappointment was all too familiar. She knew quite well that my practice was bursting with new patients and that other doctors owed me plenty of "payback" call time. I actually had plenty of time for fun and family. So she'd put together another family event—only to hear how that was not my priority.

***

"Church people" used to ask me questions like, "Why did the Jews kill Christ?" and "Did you know you're going to hell?" I was more amused than offended, unless it was someone that I didn't like. I could always joke my way out of such confrontations. It was just "beer talk."

Growing up in the so-called "Bible Belt" that is the American South, I expected people to confront me occasionally about my personal religious beliefs. As far as I could tell, they simply wanted to goad me into a debate because I was different. I came to enjoy such confrontations as a kind of competitive sport.

I had no deeply held philosophies or brilliant intellectual traps for religionists. The folks I encountered were simply unprepared to defend what they claimed to believe. They could quote Scripture verses, but they couldn't seem to discuss them or harmonize them into practical lifetime applications.

I concluded that such people robotically downloaded their memorized Bible verses into others so that they wouldn't have to explain what it was that they really believed. What they called "faith" would never hold up before reason and logic—or so I believed. I could generally out argue such people. But I could not argue or joke my way out of the challenge that a guy like Mike presented.

Like wartime, the pressures of medical school had created unlikely friendships. I became buddies with many who called themselves Christians—and some probably were. But Mike Hendren was notable. He was intellectual, articulate and clean-cut—the latter quality being an oddity in the culture of the early 70s, even in medical school.

It seemed to me like most people's religion was just a matter of adhering to the predigested propaganda preached at the church of their parent's choosing. That was not true in Mike's case. Mike's story began, in some ways, at the University of Arkansas at Fayetteville, where he had been an outstanding running back for the Arkansas Razorback football team.

I was raised on the Razorbacks. We only had one big football team in Arkansas, and we were proud of them. People followed the Razorbacks everywhere. And Mike was one of the best tailbacks Arkansas ever had. He and a linebacker named Robert Lewis had bright futures on the squad until both sustained serious injuries during a game. Their dreams and goals suddenly shattered, Mike and Robert began seeking spiritual solutions, and both ended up becoming devout followers of Jesus. Their experience was, in a sense prophetic of what happened to about 5/6 of that team, but that's a story for another chapter.

A couple of years later, Mike was a freshman in medical school. He was deeply committed to God, which is to say that he *trusted* God in ways that actually affected how he chose to live his life. If he thought God wanted him to do this or not do that, he was satisfied to live that way and not make excuses for being different. The result was, Mike was the first person of my generation whose faith made him different in a way that was appealing to me.

We often studied together. Because Mike did not "clobber" me with his religious views, I felt free to observe as he interacted with his family and as he dealt with real life issues. I was unable to explain his dependence on

God; he didn't seem to use God or religion as a "crutch" to find approval and significance, as others seemed to do. We remained friends after medical school, and I could not help comparing my life to his.

Like me, Mike had married a hometown girl and they were already raising a family. That's where the similarities ended. Mike's life was filled with peace; mine was filled with relentless activity and uncertainty. His marriage was based on commitment, mine, performance. He was self-confident; I was self-conscious.

The strange thing was, when I looked at my life, I should have been filled with peace and contentment. I had what I wanted—a family, a career—success by whatever standards I knew to measure it.

Yet as Linda put it, I was a man without peace. Sure I spent time with her and the kids occasionally, but I was not the family man I wanted to be. I was pursuing windmills relentlessly. As soon as I'd learned how to do one thing and reached the highest level of accomplishment I could, I'd go to the next thing. I needed constant challenges, continual accomplishments, almost like a drug addict looking for the next fix. That's how I dealt with my anger and frustration.

I liked to discover the extreme of any given task. For example, throughout medical school, I'd think of the most unlikely goal line, then head for it. Crossing it was consummate bliss, but the high soon faded—more so with every score, with every touchdown—until finally, my restlessness consumed me as I looked around for the next challenge.

When I did take time off, I was dedicated to the pursuit of nothing particularly worthwhile, such as flying or riding. We had a small, five-acre ranch with horses. To me, relaxing meant doing whatever I wanted, usually self-engaged types of activities.

I don't mean to imply that I didn't spend time with my family. There were so many times Linda wanted me to be with her, to be with them. I'd be late or cancel because I was busy doing something else. Sometimes doctors would be in a feud, and like my dad, I'd be there to make the peace. I became president of a 75-doctor Independent Physician Association—not because I was the smartest of all the doctors, but because I got along with everybody—like my daddy did. Like him, I got a lot of satisfaction when people would call on me in times of trouble.

Linda was probably the only one who knew of my perpetual restlessness.

And I knew. I saw my life as the antithesis of Mike Hendren's. Unlike me, he was unaffected by the waxing and waning of a self-absorbed lifestyle. His kindness and genuine affection for me were compelling. I liked being with Mike. I trusted him. I respected his opinion. I even watched my language when I was around him. He wasn't real talkative, but he had a quiet, reassuring smile. He was the one who encouraged me to go into family practice, and it turned out to be very good advice.

Mike and I shared office space, so we saw each other under real pressure, striving to be professional as we encountered life-threatening situations with our patients, while also dealing with the various personal challenges of maintaining a family. The difference was that Mike always had endless strength from which to draw, a strength that I did not understand or even desire at the time. I tried to explain it away as his "religion keeping him afloat." Yet I could not deny the power in Mike's life, a life dependent on God. How dependence could be a source of strength was beyond me—but there it was.

"How wonderful it would be," I thought, "to believe something so completely that it could fill me with self-confidence, forbearance, patience—if only!" But it was hard to admit that I needed what Mike had.

Certainly, I knew that my life had not been "perfect" by anyone's measurement. Yet like former President Richard Nixon, I could not admit my specific mistakes. He once excused his behavior after it was made public by saying, "Mistakes were made." Like him, it was difficult for me to say, "*I* made mistakes," much less enumerate them.

I didn't think of myself as "a sinner." The very word seemed archaic and extreme. I just accepted that life had thrown me a few curve balls to which I reacted with an improperly adjusted swing. To me, sin was what was wrong with other people; it was all the bad things *that I did not do*. Mine were not sins; they were "problem areas" that I would eventually, somehow, overcome. In time, I believed, I would deal with them sufficiently. How easy it is for us to see wrong in others but excuse it in our own behaviors, usually blaming it on something or someone else. That position was comfortable and seemed to work well for me for thirty-seven years.

I could excuse away my every wicked thought or act by comparing it to the wickedness of society in general. I could also make myself feel better by repeating my "I nevers": I never killed, never kidnapped, never robbed, never this and never that. Whenever some transgression caused my guilt to become overwhelming, I would simply comfort myself with a comparison. "Yes, I did that, but not as much or as often as so-and-so!"

Like many people, I reasoned that my compliance with the "standard" was at least as good as some, and better than most. If God existed, I reasoned, my position would be safe because it was very close to the median of "acceptable behavior." Surely there is safety in numbers! Isn't truth decided by majority opinion? Isn't the majority always right simply because it is the majority? Wouldn't God, if he existed, grade "on the curve"?

But my reasoning was purely according to my experiences and perceptions. It was fallible, often serving to justify my selfish actions rather than to explore truth. But sometimes when we are not in a place to go looking for the truth, the truth comes looking for us instead.

CHAPTER THIRTEEN:

CABINET DOORS

"I'll build your kitchen cabinets and I won't charge you for the labor, but I would like to spend some time talking with you—say for an hour some night?"

I knew he wanted to talk to me about his religion. If that was the price for our new cabinets, it sounded pretty good to me.

"Sure, Steve," I said. "It's a deal."

***

It was the late 70s. I needed help in the office and my transcriptionist told me about a young man named Steve Johnson whom she knew from church. Steve was working his way through undergraduate school. He was headed toward medical school and wanted whatever experience he could get in a medical office. By that time, I was comfortable around these Christian-types, so I hired Steve as a clinical assistant.

Skilled, dependable and clean-cut, his demeanor reminded me a lot of Mike. I found out Steve had "converted" and become a Christian while overseas in the military. It came as quite a surprise to me that these Gentiles "became" Christians. I thought they were born that way, just as I was born a Jew. At any rate, like Mike, Steve didn't talk much about his faith; it just seemed to come out in how he lived his life. He made rounds with me, he was very good at what he did and quite pleasant to have around the office. One day, Steve heard me discussing plans to renovate my house.

My father had bought Linda and me an absolutely huge house. By huge, I mean about 9,500 square feet, all centrally heated and air-conditioned. The house really was far too large for us. My dad enjoyed having a son who was a physician and he wanted the world to know that we had "arrived." The house was his tribute to me, and in a sense to himself. He wanted to do everything he could for me, and I didn't say no.

We needed to replace the kitchen cabinets, and I'd been on the phone with a carpenter to discuss possibilities. When I hung up, Steve said, "You need to have some cabinet work done in your kitchen?"

I said, "Yeah, I do."

Steve told me that he'd worked as a carpenter in high school and in college. Someone in the office chimed in, "Yeah, he's very good."

"Really?" I said, "Do you do cabinet work?"

He smiled. "That's my specialty."

I asked if he'd do mine, and what it would cost me. And so we struck our bargain, at least, it was a bargain for me! (I looked at some of his work, which confirmed to me that he indeed was a qualified carpenter.)

True to his word, Steve built the cabinets, and he did a fine job.

And then I dodged him.

I didn't mean to dodge him, exactly. He'd come to me and say, "Charles, do you have some time tonight?" And I'd say, "Gosh, I wish I did but I've got this or that to do, let's get together next week." And somehow, the following week, there was just as much to do—so the time never came. Until finally, one night, as I was preparing for a trip to Houston, Steve dropped by the house.

I was packing for the trip when Steve rang the doorbell. I answered and he said, "I've come to collect my hour." I explained that it wasn't a good time, that I was getting ready to leave for Houston to visit my cousin Shelley who was dying of cancer.

"Charles," he said, "I don't think I'm ever going to be able to call you, why don't we just talk?" I looked at Steve who'd held his end of the bargain so beautifully, and who had patiently waited for me to uphold mine. He had a right to be angry, but he wasn't. He'd just come to collect what I owed him. I knew an hour would not make me late, so I invited him in.

Steve didn't take much time, maybe not even the full hour he'd requested. He did not try to win me with persuasive speech, nor did he bait me with questions that were really traps. He presented his beliefs simply and gently. He had four main points.

First, he spoke of God's love for me and how God had wanted me to be his person all of these years.

Then he told me about sin. He explained that sin literally means, "to miss the mark." Because God is holy and just, all of us "miss the mark" and miss being with God, who is perfectly holy. Steve drew a diagram and showed me how, according to the Bible, missing the mark meant people were separated from God and needed to be "saved." Separation from God equals death, not just in a sense that we will physically die, but spiritual death—being cut off from God who is the source of spiritual life. This explained what I never quite grasped way back in my childhood—when I'd found my way into that revival tent and was so excited about getting saved, though I wasn't sure what it meant.

Steve's third point was that God was not satisfied with this separation, so he implemented a plan to bridge the gap. Steve explained that plan as atonement (covering for sin) through a substitute.

During Bible times, the Jewish people followed God's plan as they sacrificed animals at certain appointed times in very specific ways commanded by God. The person would put his hands upon the animal's head to symbolize his acknowledgment that sin brings death and separation—and that God allowed the death of the innocent animal to be a symbolic substitute for the spiritual death of its owner.

Steve explained that animals could not actually take the consequences of a human being's sin. The forgiveness of sin was God's gracious response to the people's faith in God. They demonstrated they believed they needed forgiveness, and they believed in God's plan of forgiveness every time they obeyed his instructions concerning these sacrifices.

Steve went on to tell me that the sacrifices did not take away people's sin; rather, it covered or atoned for their sin until the next time. This part sounded vaguely familiar to me from childhood days of celebrating the Jewish High Holy Days. Yom Kippur was also known as "The Day of Atonement." But we didn't have any sacrifices, and it was never exactly clear to me how or why God would forgive our sins.

Steve explained that there is no longer a Temple or altar by which we can approach God in that same prescribed way. Yet, he said, we all still need the atonement God made available through this plan, and God never revealed a different plan. In order to have our sin covered so we can be with God, we still needed a *substitute*, Steve said. So, (he believed), God sacrificed his son; and in so doing, he made Jesus our unblemished (sinless) lamb.

Again, the first three things Steve explained to me were: God's love for me; the fact that everyone, including me, commits sin and this sin separates me from God; and God sent the Messiah, Jesus to be an atonement for my sins.

Then came Steve's clincher. He said Jesus' blood only covers my sin when I personally surrender my life to *receive* him both as savior and as Lord. Were I to ask Jesus to be my savior, Steve explained, it would mean I wanted him to be my substitute for the penalty of my sin, for which I alone am ultimately responsible to God.

I knew from my bar mitzvah that I was supposed to be responsible to God for my sin. Ironically, no one had mentioned exactly how to shoulder this responsibility. Somehow it had never been a real cause for concern.

Nor was it particularly a cause for concern when Steve explained it. I had kept my end of the bargain. I concluded that Steve's explanation of his beliefs was fascinating, even compelling in its way. But I was not about to turn my life upside down for the sake of some interesting ideas. That was the end of it as far as I was concerned. But those kitchen cabinets had opened a door, and Steve was not going to let it close so quickly.

One day, he invited me to visit his church to hear from a young Jewish man who had been born and raised in Poland during World War II. As a youth, he had experienced hatred from so-called "Christians" who had cruelly isolated and persecuted him and his family. They justified their evil with the accusation that Jews were "Christ-Killers," and they saw it as their religious duty to punish the Jews. At first that punishment was verbal, but it turned violent. The "Christians" besieged this boy's small community, killing Jews and stealing their possessions to divide among themselves and their "religious" leaders.

That boy, Arnold Fruchtenbaum, had every reason to despise and distrust these people known only as "the Christians." Yet when the thirteen-year-old arrived as an immigrant in one of New York City's Jewish districts, he encountered a different kind of Christian. These people showed him genuine love, acceptance, compassion and a different view of Jesus. Before long, Arnold was evaluating who Jesus was apart from his traumatic childhood experiences. Eventually, he became a follower of Jesus. His superb intellect and knowledge of Judaism as well as Christianity earned him respect—and many invitations to speak at churches such as the one Steve was inviting me to attend.

Steve of course was eager to have me hear Arnold. "Hey," he said, "there's a Jewish fellow coming to our church, and I wish you'd go with me to hear him." I was not thrilled about it, but the little he told me about Arnold's story did pique my interest a bit, so I more or less agreed to go to one evening of a three-day Bible conference Arnold was teaching.

However, after a week or two had passed and it was time to go, I became reluctant. Steve and I walked out to the parking lot, and Mike Hendren showed up. But I had my ace in the hole. "Gosh Steve," I said, "you know I didn't get to make rounds this morning. I need to go back around." Mike had a great big smile and he said, "Well, I've made all your rounds for you." Mike and I shared calls from time to time, so this was not totally out of the blue—though the timing of his help was obviously no coincidence. He showed me the notes he'd made, gave me a report and demonstrated that all my patients were okay. I was without excuse.

I figured I would humor my friends—after all, no one ever died of boredom. We went across the river to a nearby Bible church. It didn't have tall steeples; it was a rather small church on a little side street. We walked into a room with maybe 125 folding chairs, nearly all of which were filled. We found three seats together in the back.

Had Arnold discussed intricate prophetic passages of the Bible that night, I would have been as bored as I expected to be. Instead, he introduced the concept of prophecy in general by explaining God's promises to Abraham and his descendants. Well, I'm a descendant of Abraham, and if God made some promises to me, I wanted to know about it.

Arnold explained that the promises are collectively known as the Abrahamic Covenant, and he pointed them out in Genesis, chapter 12. I was familiar with the word "covenant" because of my father's extensive involvement in B'nai B'rith, which literally means "sons of the covenant." I had never really thought of myself as being part of a covenant with God and found it quite interesting.

That covenant has three main points. First, God promised Abraham and all his Jewish descendants a land. Second, God promised eternal blessings for the Jewish people. Finally, God promised a special blessing for *all* peoples, by virtue of a Messiah who was also to be Jewish. These three promises, according to the Jewish Bible, are unconditional and eternal. And according to Arnold, God was saying that a descendant of Abraham, a Jew, would be the means of salvation for Jews and Gentiles.

Various chapters of succeeding human history demonstrate how God has kept his promise to the Jewish people, although history also records that many times we have not kept our promises to him.

Every nation that has set out to eradicate the Jews has ceased to exist, yet the Jews continue to thrive and now have a population estimated to be equal to any other period in our national history. Suddenly, I could see that God had dealt with the Jewish people exactly as he had promised Abraham.

"He must exist!" The thought seemed to explode in my mind. The fact that the Jewish people continue to survive was evidence enough. And just like that, any doubt I had about God's existence vanished.

That day changed my life. For the first time, I saw the value of the Bible for me personally. I had previously dismissed it as a collection of stories, ceremonial responsibilities and relics of which only a rabbi could make much sense. Now, through the Bible, I'd realized that God exists. It was too big a realization to ignore, but I wasn't sure what to do about it. I was stunned.

When Arnold's talk was over, I was invited to join a group of people who were meeting informally with Arnold in Jerry Hill's home. Jerry was one of the church deacons. Surprisingly, I found that I was eager to go.

Everyone was quite gracious to me, and many seemed to want to talk to me, but I was fairly focused in Arnold's direction. I could listen politely to my Gentile Christian friends telling about their beliefs because it was the gentlemanly, ecumenical thing to do. But if I was going to consider this Jesus seriously, for my own life, I needed to talk to another Jew.

I saw that Arnold was in conversation, but I kind of expected that he would move towards me and engage me in conversation. I knew many of the people there had been praying for me to be "saved." I felt that I was probably as much the center of attention as Arnold.

When Arnold didn't approach me, I moved toward the group where he was sitting. I got close and I was just listening to him speaking to the others. I began asking him a few guarded questions and finally I just blurted out, "Well the Bible is so extensive. How can anybody know it in a lifetime?"

That was not an uncommon Jewish viewpoint concerning the Bible. I recalled the rabbi telling me, as he awaited the birth of my younger son with me, that one does not simply read the Bible. He explained that you have to read so many years of commentaries, and only then can you possibly begin to understand the smallest portions of Scripture. So I had always assumed that reading the Bible is not a feat that average laypeople can aspire to on their own.

Arnold replied that he'd read a book that might be helpful to me, a panorama Bible study course by Alfred T. Eade. Jerry Hill, who was sitting with us brightened. "I think I've got that." He went over to a dusty old cabinet and pulled it out. "Here it is." I put the book under my coat, we talked a bit more, then I went home.

Once home, I opened that book and read and read and read until I could not read anymore. Nothing had ever been quite so compelling as this feeling of watching God at work through history. That one thought, "He really exists!" seemed to fill my mind. It was such a big thought for me, the biggest thought I'd ever had. From that point on, I continued reading.

I began researching various books about theology, comparing different religious philosophies. I began with traditional Judaism, studying it seriously and with considerable scrutiny. Then I read about Islam, as well as Hinduism and "New Age" religions. I pondered the premises of various "mother earth" philosophies. And I read about Christianity.

Surprisingly, I found myself agreeing with the late Christian apologist, C. S. Lewis. He concluded that there are really only two religious viewpoints in the world. One he calls "authentic Christianity," which acknowledges God alone as Creator of all things: a "personal" God inasmuch as he is approachable—but only through Jesus Christ.

The second, more widely accepted religion is one or another variation of the idea of an impersonal God. A variety of religions that appear totally different fall under this same umbrella. They hold in common an attitude, if not an actual doctrine, that God is something we create in our minds and not vice versa. Even those that may officially teach that God is Creator have been watered down to reflect the preferences of his supposed worshipers.

I had come to believe the reality of God and the certainty of his existence apart from me or my preferences. Beyond that, I hesitated. I didn't want to take God's existence too personally. I was afraid I might have to change. I was afraid of losing my independence (even though my "independence" consisted of selfish ambitions that controlled who I was and how I thought). I was aware that my sins (which I preferred to call faults), kept me in a comfortable place where I didn't have to worry about what God might expect.

I couldn't walk away from this newfound understanding of God, yet I didn't want to walk away from life as I knew it. I was profoundly excited by the reality—I couldn't help seeing it as reality—that one could have a real relationship with God, that it wasn't some questionable hope that may or may not materialize in an afterlife.

I was also astounded by such biblical passages as this one from Isaiah 53: "He is despised and rejected by men, a man of sorrows and acquainted with grief. And we hid, as it were, our faces from him; he was despised, and we did not esteem him. Surely he has borne our griefs and carried our sorrows; yet we esteemed him stricken, smitten by God, and afflicted. But he was wounded for our transgressions, he was bruised for our iniquities; the chastisement for our peace was upon him, and by his stripes we are healed. All we like sheep have gone astray; we have turned, every one, to his own way; and the LORD has laid on him the iniquity of us all. He was oppressed and he was afflicted, yet he opened not his mouth; he was led as a lamb to the slaughter, And as a sheep before its shearers is silent, so he opened not his mouth" (Isaiah 53:3-7).

No wonder the rabbis taught that laypeople could not hope to understand the Bible apart from their commentaries. Here were verses in the Jewish Bible that seemed to be pointing straight to Jesus.

Oddly, it wasn't only Jesus that I was waking up to—it was my own Jewishness. For the first time, I started understanding why it was meaningful to be a Jew, other than pleasing my family, who found it meaningful because they needed to please their family, and so forth.

Suddenly, as I honed in on the promise of a Jewish Messiah, I began to see our place (the place my Jewish people held) in history. Honestly, this had never made sense to me before.

I had grown up in a dual culture, and in some ways, I tended to lean more toward the non-Jewish culture. I was loyal to my family and my heritage. Nevertheless, the religious training struck me as being a little silly. Moreover, the boys I'd studied with for my bar mitzvah were not my closest friends. And while family was very important to me, I'd detected somewhat of a superiority and a sense of separateness in some of my relatives which I found unappealing.

I related closely with folks in the black community, and tended to find my closest friends among the Gentiles. It wasn't that I wanted to be a Gentile or that I wouldn't defend my Jewishness against anyone who was anti-Semitic. It's just that what I perceived as the inward-looking or parochial side of Judaism was of little interest to me.

Once I understood that being Jewish wasn't just something to elevate our self-esteem, but to help the world know God, it was as though a switch had been thrown. I learned to appreciate my Jewishness in a new way.

I tried to tell myself that all of these biblical conclusions I was reaching were intellectual. I did not wish to act on them. I tried coming up with a compromise: a hybrid of what I knew to be true and what I "wanted" to be true. But I could not place a square peg in a round hole. It didn't fit, I knew it didn't fit and eventually, I gave up trying to make it fit.

For weeks and weeks I wrestled with indecision, desperately holding on to my old life. The truth of Arnold's teachings, of the Bible, of the lives of people like Mike and Steve was pressing in on me. Finally, emotionally drained, I realized that I had to resolve the conflict once and for all.

I reasoned, "If Jesus really is the way to know God, then why would I not want him? What on earth could be more valuable? If God is findable, why should I settle for pursuing a cheap substitute (my god of achievement or success) that will rob me, when all is finished at the end of my life, of an eternal relationship with the real thing?"

As I considered my life and compared it to that of my friends, Mike and Steve, a Bible passage I'd read came to mind:

"But without faith it is impossible to please Him, for he who comes to God must believe that He is, and that He is a rewarder of those who diligently seek Him" (Hebrews 11:6).

Then came the tiebreaker. If I accepted Jesus as Messiah and Lord, the worst that could happen was that eventually I'd realize I'd been wrong and appear a little foolish for a while. That certainly would not be the first time for me. On the other hand, if I chose to ignore what I had come to believe was true—and it really was true—my eternal destiny was at stake.

I'd begun to suspect that God had been pursuing me for some time—that seemingly unrelated events were, in fact, connected to God's care for me and his plans for me to know him. This will sound incredibly self-centered, perhaps even megalomaniacal to anyone who does not have that kind of intimate relationship with God. All I can say is that it is not a reflection of my importance in the universe. It is a reflection of God's immense love and affection for his creation. That love manifests itself in very particular and individual ways to draw all kinds of people—people who need to know God—into these very personal relationships with him. The difficulty, as I'd come to realize, is that such relationships with the Creator of the universe must be on his terms, not ours.

One starry, autumn night, on the back porch of our home, I silently said yes to Y'shua's (Jesus') offer to be my savior and my Lord. I told God I wanted to follow him for the rest of my life. I climbed into bed, fell asleep easily and awoke refreshed for the first time in months.

The next day, I knew that something had taken place deep within my soul. I was not alone, nor would I ever be again. I felt a deep sense of satisfaction, comfort and peace, the kind you feel after realizing that you made a right decision and your life is never going to be the same again. In this case, it was going to be much, much better.

CHAPTER FOURTEEN:

THE RABBI VISITS

"Charles, have you got a minute?" My father sounded uncharacteristically anxious.

"Sure, Dad, anytime. What's up?"

"Listen, son," he continued, "the rabbi is on his way to Hot Springs for some arthritis treatment. His right arm, you know, has been very painful. Anyway, he would very much like to stop in Little Rock and visit with you and Linda for a few minutes."

I had been expecting this call for some time. "Sure, Dad. Tell him to drop by. We'll be expecting him," I replied. I hung up the phone and took a long, deep breath.

* * *

I had made only a single statement to Linda: "I believe that Jesus is the Messiah. I feel God changing my life because of my decision to believe in him." She didn't understand what that meant, but it sounded like a threat to our Jewish way of life. Linda had become, in many ways, a better Jew than me. She made sure we kept the kosher dietary laws, observed the Jewish holidays and festivals and she raised our four children according to Jewish tradition. She was even among a small group who organized a successful effort to start the first Jewish day school in Little Rock. She was not thrilled to hear that I believed in Jesus.

At the same time, she was confused by the changes she saw in me. I was no longer rushing here and there to do extraneous things as before. I was more settled and peaceful, and she didn't know what to make of it. Instead of taking off in my plane or going out riding, I would go off to the den and read. At times I'd just sit there, apparently doing nothing. (I was praying, but as most Jewish prayer is done from a set prayer book, Linda had no way of knowing what I was doing.)

Whereas she used to worry about my restlessness, at least she understood it. It was a familiar paradigm. Suddenly she felt she no longer understood the rules. She saw me leaving books like *Jesus Was a Jew* on the kitchen counter. And it scared her. She was afraid for our relationship—not because of how I related to her, but because she was not where I was spiritually, and she wasn't sure how to relate to me. She didn't know what to do. So she called Dad.

She and Dad had become very close. She told him that I was reading Christian books and I was changing. It's not that the changes were bad, but they indicated that Christianity somehow had a hold on me. The two of them secretly conspired to dissuade me from a "religion" that had always left her empty.

Their strategy was for Linda to simply read what I was reading and then to reason with me. They assumed it would be easy for her to show me where I had missed the meaning and the message of the life of Jesus. She would be the expert who had already rejected Christianity and could show me why I ought to do the same.

And so Linda began to read. She read *Jesus Was a Jew*, then she began reading part of the New Testament. As Linda began equipping herself to confront me, a strange change began in her life as well. Her soul became restless. She began waking up in the middle of the night and pacing the floor. I never knew why. Night after night she would secretly read the Bible. Instead of becoming fortified in her opinion that Jesus was nonsense, the opposite happened. She became irresistibly drawn to Jesus, though her purpose in reading was to push him out of both our lives.

Linda began to discover Bible passages with meanings that she had never before noticed. These words promised her forgiveness, security and new life. She started to understand that the changes she saw in me were because I had found those very things.

One day when the children were in school, she got in the car and drove to Conway, which is about 30 miles northwest of Little Rock. She drove up and down the highway, just trying to process all her thoughts. Jesus was making sense to her, but she didn't know what to do with it. She was thinking, "Will somebody tell me what to do?" without even realizing it was a prayer.

I was not at home that night. I had late rounds because I had some people in the emergency room. For some reason, Steve came and knocked on the door that evening. It was only the second time he'd been by our house since making the cabinets. Linda asked him, "What has happened with Charles? He's different."

Steve replied, "Well, let me show you." He drew the same diagrams that he'd drawn for me: the two cliffs, the chasm that sin has made between God and humanity, and the bridge God provided through Jesus. Linda prayed with Steve, then she cried.

By the time I came home, it must have been 1:00 a.m. I found Linda missing from our bedroom. I searched the house for several minutes and finally spotted her through the kitchen window. She was outside on the back porch, clad in her nightgown and bathrobe, her lean figure silhouetted by the early morning moonlight. Quietly drawing closer, I peered at her through the glass. Her lips were moving in silent prayer; her eyes were filled with tears which spilled onto the Bible she'd been reading.

I walked outside quietly so as not to interrupt her, just to see what was going on. After a few moments, she saw me. She started crying again, and she said, "Oh, Charles, I believe too." And then she reached up to hug me. We just held each other for a long time.

At that time, we really didn't have any Christian friends except for Mike and Steve. We realized that in order to grow we needed to associate ourselves with other believers. I knew of a group called "Jews for Jesus"— in fact one of their missionaries had visited me when he was passing through Little Rock. I was not interested in the gospel at the time, and made sure it was a pretty brief visit. In fact, you might say I threw him out—though in a polite, southern kind of way.

Mike Hendren told us about a new church in town, Fellowship Bible Church, and I was intrigued. The story of Fellowship Bible Church could probably be a book in itself. It starts with a football game in 1969. Some considered it one of the greatest football games in the history of American football: the Arkansas Razorbacks versus the Texas Longhorns. At the time, Texas was number one in the nation and Arkansas was number two.

I saw that game. It was such a big game that Richard Nixon came down from Washington as did many political dignitaries. Arkansas was wiping its perennial rival all over the field that Saturday afternoon, though we were not that far ahead of them on the scoreboard. Yet with just minutes to go, we had them beat; in fact, I already saw people celebrating. Then incredibly, the ball passed right through the hands of the Razorbacks into the arms of the Longhorns who, against all odds, scored and won.

That night was like a funeral at the University of Arkansas; there was a pall over the whole city. The next morning, some four or five guys on the squad who were Christians got up and went to church. Those few guys seemed to be doing okay, but the rest of the Razorbacks weren't. Over the next weeks, the guys who were Christians were having Bible studies. Other players started dropping in to see what they were doing; what they had that enabled them to cope with the loss. And something incredible happened, which I don't believe ever happened before or since. Out of 120 men on the football team, around 100 of them became Christians. And over the next three years, about 30–35 of them became ministers—a fourth of the football team.

Fellowship Bible Church was an outgrowth of that phenomena. One of the pastors, Robert Lewis, had been a linebacker on the team. A couple of the original elders were teammates.

The church had a friendly, casual atmosphere and the pastor really knew how to communicate. Nevertheless, it was a bit lonely—because, as I once remarked to my wife, "We may be the only Jews in the south who believe in Jesus."

Then just four weeks into our "adventure," along came the Sternbergs.

We were not prepared for the Sternbergs—no, not at all prepared. Jack Sternberg is a medical oncologist in Little Rock with impressive credentials from the M.D. Anderson Clinic in Houston, Texas, and an equally impressive residency training at the Cleveland Clinic in Cleveland, Ohio. In Cleveland, Jack met and married Marilyn Meckler, a very energetic Jewish woman.

Jack's a big six-footer from Brooklyn, with lots of savvy and self-confidence. He can intimidate with just a glance. He knows his medicine;

at hospital conferences he has been known to "run the table" when challenged on points of medical expertise. He's not anyone that you want to tangle with unless you are comfortable being decisively outdone. Many an up-and-coming young intellectual has found himself in over his head when stepping forward to challenge Jack. Older ones have fared just as poorly.

I didn't know Jack well. Little Rock is somewhat of a provincial place, and while I was not ashamed to be Jewish, I was a very different Jew (in my estimation) from Jack. This guy was a New Yorker. He talked like a New Yorker, he interrupted like a New Yorker and as far as I was concerned, it was loud, ill-mannered, argumentative Yankees like him who gave the rest of us Jews a bad name. Now, having said that, it may seem odd, but I also greatly admired Jack. He was likable (in a northern sort of way), and he was brilliant. I just wasn't looking to be closely associated with him. So it was something of a surprise when he pulled into my driveway one fall afternoon as I was mowing the grass.

Sticking his hand out of his big sports utility vehicle, he asked me, "Want a cold soda pop?"

"Sure," I replied, taking the drink from his extended hand.

We chatted for a while. Jack mentioned that he'd brought a new partner into his practice and asked me to think about referring him some patients. He continued chatting as my mind wandered a bit. Then I sensed an inner voice softly urging me, "Tell him about Jesus!"

"What!" I almost shouted out loud. "No way!" I thought to myself. "I do not want to have a lengthy conversation with Jack Sternberg about anything, much less to tell him about my spiritual journey."

Even so, I was amazed to hear myself say, "Jack, you know, I've been reading about the life and claims of Jesus Christ. I believe he's our Messiah. I think we Jews have missed it."

Now the truth is, I was so thrilled with my discovery that I expected anyone I might choose to share it with to be equally thrilled. I'd hesitated to tell Jack because this was something rather personal, and that was not the type of relationship we had. Since I had gone ahead and blurted it out, I was prepared to discuss it further.

Jack was not. I'd only gotten about two sentences out of my mouth before Jack was laying down some pretty thick rubber on his way off my property, yelling, "See ya later!" in his after smoke.

I realized Jack was offended, and I felt rejected. The fact that I wasn't seeking a relationship with Jack didn't matter. I wasn't used to being rejected and I didn't plan to make a habit of it. I thought, "Okay Lord, I'm yours for life as I promised, but you'll have to find someone else to be your front man because I'm never going to open myself up to such humiliation again."

Two weeks later, around nine o'clock on a Saturday night, the phone rang. I answered it and was surprised to hear Jack's voice on the other end. Caught off guard, I braced for the onslaught.

Jack sounded very cautious, "Charles, you guys aren't going to a church now, are you?"

I answered carefully, not wanting to give much information, "Yes, Jack, we are."

Never comfortable with preliminaries, Jack cut to the chase. "Can Marilyn and I go with you tomorrow?"

It was the nearest thing to a miracle that I'd ever heard! (Later I realized that our daughter, Alison, was friends with their daughter, Jennifer, and had mentioned needing to be home early Saturday night because she had to get up early the next morning to go to church.)

The following morning, we met the Sternbergs at church, which at that time was only about 200 people meeting in a school gymnasium. They seemed enthralled by the message and overwhelmed by the warmth of the congregation, who welcomed them as if they had known them forever. Afterwards, they insisted on coming to our house where they demanded that we immediately download everything we knew, which wasn't much. But, we tried.

Particularly exciting to them were the messianic prophecies from the Jewish Bible; predictions that pointed to the birth, life and crucifixion of Jesus of Nazareth. These prophecies predated the actual events by as many as a thousand years; yet they had been fulfilled in history with utmost exactitude, to the smallest letter.

Over several evenings throughout the next few weeks, Linda and I shared everything we knew about Christianity with Jack and Marilyn. It quickly became obvious to us that we were about to outrun our supply lines. Years later, they both told us it was not so much the information we shared that led them to explore Jesus for themselves; rather, they said, it was the contentment they saw in us as well as the confidence about our eternal well-being we seemed to exude. Our lives led them to examine and compare the relative emptiness of their own outwardly successful lives.

Jack and Marilyn spent months studying the Scriptures for themselves and visiting our church, where they continued to experience love and acceptance. They asked sincere questions, the kind that people ask when they are really in search of something. Finally, they reached a point where they realized it was time to either accept that Jesus was true or else dismiss him once and for all as fiction, and get on with the rest of their lives.

So, when they learned that the rabbi was coming for a visit, they asked if they could join us. They were nearing the end of their truth-seeking quest, and when Jews seek spiritual truth they usually want to hear what the rabbi thinks. He is considered the fount of knowledge out of which springs all truth about the Torah and God.

It was about that time that I finally told my father, "You know, Dad, we're Christians." I told him that Linda believed as well, and she also talked to him about it. That really troubled Dad since he was counting on her to dissuade me. It was also the first time I used the word Christian rather than simply saying believer in Jesus—which is what Christian means to me. But "Christian" meant something else to Dad. "How can you be Gentile?!" he exclaimed.

I knew that between my two parents, it would be much more difficult trying to explain this to Dad. I didn't expect my mother to agree, but I knew I could count on her empathy. No one has ever heard my mother say a disparaging word about another human being. She is an extremely active listener and feels the emotions others express very deeply. She has not a manipulative bone in her body. Not that my father would ever intend to manipulate me. But he would do whatever he could to make things right, as he understood right.

I tried explaining that I was still Jewish. He was desperate—he didn't want his grandchildren to be Christians, or Gentiles, as he believed they would become—and before long I got the call asking if the rabbi could stop in and see us.

The whole thing had to be orchestrated. My dad was in Forrest City, the rabbi was in Memphis, which is one hour east of Forrest City. We were in

Little Rock, an hour and a half west of Forrest City. Hot Springs is about an hour west of Little Rock. However, I don't think the rabbi was on his way to Hot Springs.

This was an Orthodox rabbi, a very learned leader of a congregation in a large metropolitan, multi-cultural city. His family tree was laden with generations of rabbis and Jewish scholars. In addition to his rabbinic credentials, his extensive educational experience included postgraduate work in psychology.

He had considerable experience in dealing with the occasional "wayward" son or daughter of a Jewish family who had been "proselytized away" from the tradition. His expressed opinion was that Christians make certain, deliberate misinterpretations concerning the Jewish Scriptures to mislead vulnerable Jewish people into believing that the "Old Testament" (a term which many Jewish people find offensive) points to Jesus as the Messiah. He was considered particularly skillful at correcting these "mistakes."

This was perfect timing for the Sternbergs. They were very interested in Jesus and felt they needed to make a choice one way or the other. They saw the rabbi's visit as the perfect opportunity to hear "the other side" from a Jewish expert. When they asked if they could come, I almost wished I hadn't told them. I felt I needed to talk to the rabbi to satisfy my father— but what if he turned the Sternbergs away from the gospel? I think in the back of my mind, I wondered if I might have missed something, if the rabbi might point out a flaw in my own thinking and conclusions about Jesus. It had taken me a long time to admit that Jesus was for me. When I did, he changed my life—for the better. I did not want to change back.

The rabbi arrived on a moonless autumn evening. I was only mildly surprised when I saw the headlights of Dad's car easing up the driveway with Cross at the wheel. Apparently, Dad had decided to provide transportation for the rabbi. I greeted him at the front door and welcomed him inside, careful not to touch his right arm, which he held close to his breast in an arm-sling. Jack and I exchanged glances, we had never known a sling to be treatment for arthritis.

We started with the usual pleasantries. At first, the rabbi seemed to be sizing us up, particularly Jack and Marilyn, whom he did not know or expect to see.

"Are you Christians, too?" he asked.

"No." Jack said.

He seemed pleased by this response, then settled in for what he probably expected would be an evening where he would teach and we would learn, then follow his wisdom and instruction.

He began by establishing his credentials, telling us he'd come from some 53 generations of rabbis. He also explained that he had expertise in psychology and sociology. He'd studied under some rather well known people in the field. I didn't recognize their names, but Jack, who had a minor in psychology, nodded knowingly. My feeling was the rabbi was letting us know, "Hey, I'm not just a religious authority—I also know about life. I know about people."

That evening, we experienced five hours of some of the liveliest discussion in which I have ever participated. We did not intend to debate, but we wanted to know his views on specific issues that are critical to the case for Christianity.

We asked, "Do you believe Jesus ever lived?"

"No," he said.

I am guessing that he did not actually doubt the historicity of Jesus, but that he just didn't want to talk about it. But that answer did not add to his credibility that night.

We asked, "On what basis have the rabbis agreed that our ancient sages had the authority to view the Talmud, a commentary on the Bible, as having equal weight with the Bible itself?"

We continued our questions, "Weren't the first Christians Jewish?"

"How do rabbis explain the prophecies that predict major events about the life and times of Jesus? What about the ones that were fulfilled down to the smallest detail?"

The rabbi listened quietly at first, occasionally furrowing his brow to indicate incredulity that four Jews could be asking such questions. He seemed surprised that we wouldn't know better. Eventually, he switched from a passive role into a more active, angry one. "Every word of Torah is written with the blood of martyred Jews," he shouted. (Never mind that the Torah came long before Jesus walked the earth.) "Jews went to their deaths at the hands of Christians who blamed us for the death of Christ!" By now he was out of his chair and waving his arms. (Jack and I were somewhat amazed by the full range of motion in his "bad arm," which was no longer in its sling.)

He called us "disrespectful apostates," beguiled, willing "crossovers" to the side of those who hated the Jews. "You should be ashamed of yourselves. The blood of every martyred Jew is on your hands! The whole Christian theology is built on a myth; the so-called prophecies of Christ are deliberate misrepresentations of the Scriptures." He even told us that we were going to hell if we did not turn back, which we thought was strange because as far as we knew, traditional Judaism neither teaches nor believes in a doctrine of hell as a literal, actual place of eternal torment.

That was for openers; then the conversation really got interesting. This rabbi bargained with us, chided us, mocked us and generally challenged us to come back to traditional Judaism. It began to occur to us that he was not interested in exploring "biblical truth" with us; he was passionately trying to win us back from what he thought had been cultic brainwashing by anti-Semites.

Jack pointed out that we were not rebellious star-struck, drug-dazed teens of the 60s looking for "peace, love and harmony." We were professional families with reasonably stable lives who did not need or have energy to chase foolish philosophical fabrications—myths.

Jack, who still wasn't convinced about Jesus, asked, "What could our angle possibly be, rabbi? We have everything to lose and nothing to gain by taking up with some cult harboring anti-Jewish sentiment. Charles and I have a number of Jewish patients who trust us, rely on us and depend upon our professional counsel. Why would we risk these important relationships for foolishness?"

Jack was right. Our medical practices were filled and our lives exciting enough. If Jesus wasn't real, why would we waste our precious time?

Throughout our discussion, I sensed that something was missing and apparently Jack did too. Simultaneously, we realized the missing piece. The rabbi never spoke of God. For hours we had been discussing religion, heaven, earth, tradition, responsibility and Jewish contributions to modern life. Yet the rabbi had not mentioned God—not once. It's as if we had gotten together to discuss the merits, or lack thereof, of religious philosophies and historical atrocities, but God wasn't on the rabbi's agenda.

Jack—who had come with an open mind if the rabbi could show why it was foolish to believe in Jesus—was not satisfied to leave God out of the conversation. He asked the rabbi point blank why he didn't mention God in his conversation. The rabbi changed the subject on more than one occasion due to Jack's persistence. He simply was not there to address our spiritual interests and concerns.

When we asked him our most crucial question, we received a very unexpected answer. For Jews who have more than a passing interest in the Bible, the question remains: what about the requirement for an animal sacrifice for forgiveness of sin? The Bible clearly states that such a substitute was necessary: *"For the life of the flesh is in the blood, and I have given it to you upon the altar to make atonement for your souls; for it is the blood that makes atonement for the soul"* (Leviticus 17:11). This is not an isolated text; it is the capsulated explanation for many of the requirements outlined in the Torah.

We asked the rabbi, "Since the Second Temple was destroyed by the Romans in A.D. 70, where is our atonement?" If Jesus is not our lamb, then where are our substitutes now? Who has permitted us to approach God by a way other than the way God so clearly required? The rabbi sidestepped this issue without much comment—as though it were of little or no consequence.

He'd started by asking how we could believe such nonsense as the gospel and had progressed to "how dare we" believe it. In the end, he said that if there were more Jews like the four of us, we could bring Judaism back to Little Rock. He liked our spirit, our persistence. We just lacked proper guidance, he felt.

"You know," he said, "the local rabbi here is very weak. If I could have you study the Bible with me...in fact I'll tell you what I'll do...I'll come here twice a month and we'll do a Bible study. When we get through, we're going to start a new kind of Judaism that is going to shake this whole community." Those were his closing words, other than a friendly goodbye, and a thank you for allowing him to visit.

After he left late that night (it was actually about one o'clock the following morning), we all turned to look at one another. The Sternbergs were grinning, and Linda and I were too. We were all very excited. I think we hugged. It was a real bonding experience for the four of us. A new awareness had settled upon each of us. We sensed that God had been there with us, guiding us through a necessary transition in our faith journey. We'd learned that truth is not necessarily traditional, comfortable and safe—but it is beautiful and worth pursuing, whatever the cost.

For Linda and me, our faith was strengthened. When I realized the rabbi was not even concerned with the spiritual matters that had so deeply affected us, much less able to address them, it was as though the final piece had fallen into place.

The visit affected Jack and Marilyn in a similar way. Shortly after that meeting, they realized without a doubt that their quest for truth and meaning had led them to Jesus.

CHAPTER FIFTEEN:

DOCTORING DAD

"Charles, Mr. Louis looks bad. He's lying on the floor holding his chest!" My grip on the telephone tightened but it only took a second for the urgency in Cross's voice to spur me into action.

"Cross, call an ambulance to take him across the river to Memphis. I'll start heading that way." Cross had all but raised me and was like a son to Dad. Why hadn't he already called for help? After all, I was 120 miles away!

Cross, pleading now, answered my unspoken question. "I tried Charles, but he says he's not going anywhere until you get here and take care of him."

Knowing Dad's resolve when he makes up his mind, I replied, "Tell him to hold on! I'm coming. Meet me at the airport in an hour or so!"

Racing down the expressway to the airport, I called Central Flying Service from my car and asked the operations manager to quickly pull my airplane out onto the ramp. "Make sure the tanks are topped off and the engine oil checked," I added. Then I called Flight Service and filed an instrument flight plan direct to West Memphis at the lowest available altitude.

I pulled up to the ramp, jumped out of my car and ran to the airplane. My heart pounding, I climbed into the pilot seat and strapped in. The engine roared to life with the first ignition effort. The old Bonanza leaped into the cool night air in the first 1,800 feet; then it climbed "like a homesick angel" into the moon-filled sky as departure control granted my request for direct routing.

Low cloud cover darkened the landing field in West Memphis upon my arrival. Only the beacon and runway lights guided me down to the runway. I landed the airplane and took the first turnoff to the gate. Cross flashed his headlights. I taxied up to his car near the entry gate and shut the engine down.

The situation was worse than I had expected. Dad was pale, clammy and hungry for air; sweat was pouring from his skin. "Dad," I demanded, "this is crazy! Why didn't you let Cross take you to Memphis?"

Rolling his eyes towards me, his silence answered my question; he only trusted me to look after him when things got desperate and he was afraid.

Looking directly into his face, I said, "If you refuse to go to Memphis, I'll take you to Little Rock, but your job is to stay alive until we get there."

He smiled weakly and replied, "I'm not going to Memphis. I'd rather go to Little Rock where you can take care of me."

No one was around to help me lift him into the airplane; Cross was unable to lift above his knees because of chronic back problems. I put Dad on my shoulder as Cross pretty much shoved me up the first step. Finally, I muscled Dad up and across the wing and into the passenger seat. I strapped him in and patted his shoulder, then I stopped for a moment to catch my breath.

We flew just above the trees. I knew that Dad's already compromised heart muscle, by now oxygen starved, would not withstand the higher altitudes. Topping Crowley's Ridge, Dad reached over to take my hand. "Look, son," he said, "there's Forrest City." In a strange sort of way, he seemed to be enjoying the ride.

His level of alertness surprised me. I assured him, "You're going to be all right, Dad. Just keep hanging on."

He smiled and closed his eyes. His breathing eased. That's when I knew he was going to make it; this night would not be our last one together.

Fifty miles outside of Little Rock, I notified approach control that we had a medical emergency and requested a straight-in approach to the nearest active runway. This time we had help to get Dad from the plane and into my car. The cardiologist met us at the hospital emergency department. A few hours later, Dad was on the operating table getting coronary artery bypass grafting. He had almost 100 percent blockage of three major vessels and just a trickle of blood down a fourth one. He barely survived the ordeal, which was to be the first of several during the next fifteen years.

* * *

One of the most difficult and delicate scenarios in all of medicine is a physician providing medical care for his family. Good teamwork is crucial to good medicine. An over-involved family professional can actually interfere with a good medical team. Non-related physicians can be more objective, particularly about decisions that may hold increased risk to life and limb.

Strange things can occur when physicians treat their own family members. For example, it is well known that doctors' families often present clinically with weird diseases; things we don't commonly see. Our families frequently experience strange and unexpected complications to conventional medical and surgical interventions.

Some doctors become convinced that their family members have some strange, exotic illness. They have been known to draw upon the resources of the entire medical community in search of a diagnosis that never materializes. Colleagues seem unable to provide the necessary reassurances that everything is going to be okay.

Consider too, the situation in which a physician's family member has an unexpected medical complication. Suddenly, everyone becomes very conservative, sometimes too much so. All of us hesitate to order a dramatic chemical intervention with a drug that has an excellent chance to be effective, but at the same time is known to be toxic. That's when we consider the risk-to-benefit aspect of the treatment, then strive to enlist patient cooperation through informed consent.

Sometimes a drug that is known to be less effective but which also has less possibility of side effects may be substituted because the treating physician is "nervous" about a hostile family situation should the treatment have undesirable side effects. In this case, I have seen patients "watched to death" as it becomes increasingly obvious that the safer, though less effective, drug is not doing the job. Finally, at the last minute, a stronger, more effective drug may be substituted, but it may be too little, too late. Every doctor has his own story to tell at one time or another.

Once, when Dad had a dangerous post-operative infection common to diabetics, he contracted a deadly bacterium. He received a "safe" drug (possibly because he was my father) and almost died when his condition deteriorated to the point of congestive heart failure and septic shock. Without consulting others, I changed his drug to the "riskier" one and he started improving within hours of the first dose. The other doctors were probably awaiting my consent to do just that, or so I reasoned at the time.

During that episode, I was also providing medical care for my Uncle Jack in the intensive care unit. Jack was near death from a hemorrhagic stroke. I thought I was holding up pretty well, considering all that was at stake. The next morning, both of them were improved, but I awoke with Bell's Palsy—which took about three months to completely subside—from the stress.

Show me a situation where a doctor participates in the diagnosis and management of a family member's treatment and I'll show you a case in which I do not want to be involved. In Dad's case, however, I had little choice, particularly when he ignored his doctor's excellent advice and insisted that I intervene. Many times, a frustrated specialist would call me and say, "Charlie, I can't seem to get across to your Dad what's going on here and what needs to be done. Will you come help?" Overall, though, I'd say it is not really an advantage to have a doctor in the family.

The nursing staff (understandably) usually hates dealing with the doctor and his family. They prefer that the related physician keep his distance, and they sure don't want to see a doctor's family receiving advantages over other patients they are managing, such as requesting private rooms out of the normal rotational waiting list, asking for bedside attention beyond what is called for by the clinical situation, exceptional visitation privileges and so forth.

During the 12 years that Dad was near death, I found myself at the center of each one of these problems. Although it was never my intention to be difficult, when it's your family, you do what you feel you have to do. That's the truth of it. No matter how inconvenient or potentially embarrassing it may be to a colleague, you may even have to insist they stop and switch procedures in mid-stream. Because no matter how good a physician may be, she or he is only one person, and there is only so much time in the day. Mistakes happen; we have all made them despite our best efforts to be perfect in our patient care. A physician watching out for a family member is very aware of the potential for mistakes.

Once, when Dad was living in Memphis, he was hospitalized to improve control of his diabetes and to evaluate his chronic dizziness. He knew his doctor socially and his doctor knew that Dad had not been particularly compliant about taking his medication. The doctor humored Dad's complaints by hospitalizing him, if for no other reason than to keep him from phoning the office too much.

After a few days, I had not heard from Dad, which was unusual, so my daughter, Ali and I flew to Memphis to cheer him up a bit. Upon our arrival, I found Dad being loaded onto a gurney; he was hollow-eyed and near stupor.

"What's going on?" I asked the nurse.

"He's having a stroke," the nurse replied, obviously annoyed that I was interrupting her work. "The doctor just made rounds. Your dad staggered and fell this morning so the doctor ordered that he be sent to radiology for a brain scan."

Even from ten feet away, it was obvious to me that Dad was severely dehydrated, which is not an uncommon condition for insulin-dependent diabetics when they take sick. Dad's heart was straining to provide enough output to satisfy his metabolic needs.

"Call the doctor and tell him to come and re-examine Dad," I demanded. "He needs immediate fluid replacement. He's not having a stroke; he's volume depleted!"

The nurse gave me "the look"—the kind that told me she questioned from which life form I'd evolved, or that she was about to make some personal recommendations for my lunch menu choices. I presume she saw the determination in my body language, because she summoned Dad's doctor to come at once. The doctor arrived a few minutes later, visibly upset.

I spoke gently, letting him off the hook, as I hoped someone would do for me in a similar situation. "Look at his tongue and mucus membranes. They're like dried leather," I said.

Impatiently, he proceeded to the bedside and slipped his forefinger into Dad's mouth, then "unstuck" his eyelids to pull them apart. Red faced, he straightened his posture, threw me a slight nod and told the nurse, "Hurry.

Get some IV saline and run it wide open. Cancel the brain scan."

I didn't consider his misdiagnosis to be incompetence; we're all too busy. Sometimes we awake in the middle of the night worrying about whether or not we may have inadvertently neglected someone the previous day; sadly, that is occasionally the case.

Over the years, I tried to get Dad to put himself under the management of another doctor. But whenever he would develop an acute illness, I got the call. To be honest, I've done a lot of soul searching and can finally admit that I am glad he felt that way. Those times were absolutely the closest—the times we seemed the most able to communicate our love for each other. It was rare for us to actually say the words, "I love you," but we both knew.

Whenever Dad needed me, I had the opportunity to do what is hard for a son to do with his father—to sit beside him, touch him and look deep into his eyes. It's the tragedy of our human condition that, often, such extreme circumstances must occur in order to provide these kinds of father-son interactions.

Once during his long years of illness, Dad and I drove out to the airport together. I used to fly him to his B'nai B'rith engagements after it became more difficult for him to get around by himself. He enjoyed flying with me. By this time, a stroke had narrowed his visual fields, crippled his gait and left him with trembling hands. But on this particular afternoon, I strapped him into the pilot's seat of the Cessna 210 and climbed in on the passenger side next to him. Then I placed intercom-equipped headsets on both of our heads.

Taxiing into position on the runway, I requested and was permitted to fly at low altitude, close to the river around the ponds and rice fields. After reaching altitude and "trimming her off," I took my hands off the controls and announced, "Okay, Dad, you've got the airplane."

Dad was tentative at first; he cautiously moved his hands upward and forward to embrace the controls, like a man who has purchased an expensive piece of jewelry and is examining its every detail. For two hours, we carved gentle turns in the dense air over the Arkansas River valley, Dad's face occasionally broadening into a wide smile. For a time, the sparkle that had been missing for so long returned to his eyes. How precious are those times when everything is just right between a son and his father!

Despite his insistence on my personal care, Dad still gave me a hard time. Something was always "wrong" with every doctor whom I recruited to help manage his health. He always ended up back under my care with complicated conditions requiring specialist management. While he seldom admitted to me that he was satisfied with my treatment plan or the clinical outcome, he told everybody else that he was; that was his way. He'd tell me indirectly, instead of telling me himself, that he was pleased with my advice.

In fact, he constantly talked about his son the doctor, until no one could stand to hear about it anymore. Sometimes I felt resented by family and friends who were closest to him. It was as if he was making me out to be the Louis Barg he couldn't be anymore because of age and infirmity.

Although he never let anyone else provide care for him when he was sick, Dad would still discount my professional opinions. He eventually did as I instructed him, but only after I was uncompromisingly firm.

But he was never too ill or incapacitated to cease discounting anything I might say. For example, I might tell him, "Dad, your doctor in Memphis said that your diabetes is out of control." Then he would respond, "No, that's not really true. Label Katz in New Orleans has been on insulin for twenty years, since we joined B'nai B'rith together and went to the first, international, triennial convention in Israel in 1953, which was just before I went in as District President at the Galveston convention . . . et cetera, et cetera . . . and he's almost blind now and I can see great. So you see son, it's not that my diabetes is not in good control as you say, it's just that my sugar is too high."

On rare occasions, Dad would listen to what I'd say, then agree, first pass. On those occasions, he'd listen to my honest assessment of his emergent circumstances, then he'd say, "Okay, Son. Whatever you think." Those were the times that I felt the absolute closest to him, and they are among the sweetest memories of my father that I carry today.

CHAPTER SIXTEEN:

REALITIES

"Mr. Barg, are you *comfortable?*" The nurse was rolling Dad out of the post-operative recovery area following major heart surgery. She paused momentarily when she saw us standing in the corridor. She fluffed his pillow nervously and repeated her question.

Dad's eyes were still somewhat glazed from the anesthetic as he lay, looking rather lifeless, on the gurney. Slowly raising his eyelids to look her straight in the face, he replied in a weak voice, "I make a living." He shrugged his shoulders for emphasis.

We practically fell down laughing right there in the hallway. The nurse didn't get it, but laughed anyway because it seemed appropriate and because it was good to see the strain leave our faces for awhile.

***

Dad managed to stay alive some ten to fifteen years beyond what many fine doctors expected—in part, because he was usually quick to head for help whenever he felt something was really wrong. Also, he trusted my judgment and allowed me to make medical decisions for him whenever he faced special procedures, surgeries, medication changes and the like. He needed someone to be firm with him, someone who refused to be intimidated by his bluster. Once Dad realized that you had his number, he'd more or less comply peacefully.

I spoke with Dad about my belief in Jesus whenever the opportunity presented itself, and sometimes when it didn't. Even in his weakened state, Dad maintained the strength of his convictions, which often didn't seem so much heartfelt as reactionary when it came to Jesus. Predictably, he completely discounted my experience from the beginning and hoped that meeting with the rabbi—as mentioned—would straighten me out.

When Dad inquired about that interaction, I explained my problems with the rabbi's position and how he didn't seem to grapple with the issues that had led me to my conclusions. Dad let it rest—for awhile. Eventually he called and said, "The rabbi wants another opportunity to speak with you. There were important points he neglected to include when he last spoke with you." I agreed to drive to Memphis and meet with the rabbi again, but only if Dad would go with me and listen to our dialogue for himself.

He agreed and together we went to the rabbi's home. By then, I knew more about Jewish history and more about Jesus. The rabbi was very gracious and hospitable throughout our lengthy visit, but he really had nothing new to add—except concerning the subject of "substitutionary atonement" (the theological term for the sacrificial system outlined in the Torah). Why God chose to do things that way is another topic, but if he did is not debatable—it's clearly written in the Jewish Bible. So I was amazed when the rabbi announced that *he had never heard of this system*, adding, "I do not know of a time in our history when the Jews offered sacrifices for forgiveness of sin!"

It is hard to believe that he was discounting the clear teaching of the Torah—in particular the book of Leviticus. I would hate to think that he simply counted on the assumption that I hadn't read it for myself and didn't know better. Whatever his thoughts or reasons, it was, and still is to me, an amazing statement.

The rabbi's main point seemed to be that any Jew who believes in Jesus is giving up all claim to being Jewish—forever. That is the trump card that this rabbi did not hesitate to pull from his deck. But this idea reduces being Jewish to a club or a society whose members decide who is in and who is out. I was already convinced about the birth of the Jewish people as chronicled in the Bible where we see how God dealt first with Abraham, Isaac and Jacob, and made aforementioned promises to their descendants. I am one of those descendants and according to that biblical qualification, I will always be a Jew.

I told the rabbi I understood his disagreement with my beliefs, but that biblically speaking, he was on shaky ground if he considered me to be anything other than Jewish. Neither his opinions or the opinions of a million more can change the Bible, or my ancestry. That's the reality.

During the drive home, Dad was silent for a long while. Finally, he said, "Well, Son, thanks for going. You handled yourself pretty good back there; you seemed to know what you were talking about." That statement alone was worth the drive to another state.

Occasionally, Dad would visit a church to hear me teach an overview of Jewish history or tell about my personal story of faith. He even boasted to his friends about my abilities as a public speaker, telling them that his son studied the Bible and was very "religious." Word of that usually got back to me.

Once, he went with me to a luncheon of Baptist ministers. After my time of sharing with them (which included a tribute to him for his devotion to our family), Dad received pats on the back from all of the ministers. I watched him enjoying the social aspect of the gathering.

Dad had nothing against Christians or even Christianity; he had done his best to dissuade me for just one reason: we were Jewish.

His attitude toward my faith, in some ways, paralleled his response to my relationship with Linda. As a Jewish parent, he felt it his duty to dissuade me from anything that would threaten that identity—such as marrying "out." And when I would not be dissuaded, he knew that he was not supposed to tolerate my choice. Thus, when Linda and I were married we were "personas non grata."

After a time, Dad and Mom came to accept that Linda was good for me, in fact the best thing for me. And when she converted, they realized that not only was I a better person for marrying her, but she was not a threat to my Jewishness as they had believed.

With Jesus, once again Dad was duty bound to try to dissuade me because of the threat he felt my faith posed to my Jewish identity, and therefore to that of his descendants. And again, after observing changes in my life, Dad could not deny that Jesus was good for me. I'm not saying that he was happy about my faith. However, he saw it was an important part of the person I was becoming—and perhaps more to the point, that it hadn't turned me into a Gentile as he had first insisted.

In fact, Dad saw that the whole Bible had become very important to me and that I seemed to know more about Judaism than he did. Our interaction with the rabbi, while not producing the outcome he hoped for, had impressed Dad. Sometimes when matters of faith or the Bible came up with his B'nai B'rith friends, Dad would tell them, "You should talk to my son. His belief in Jesus may be a little strange but he knows a lot about Judaism and the Bible."

About once a year, I used to take an extra hour for lunch, drive to my parents' condominium, and tell them about Y'shua, hoping they would connect it with their own need to find peace with God. They always listened attentively, particularly when I spoke about the last days of human history, as we know it, and the return of the Messiah. They both believed, as do many older Jews, that the *Meshiachg gekumen* (Messiah will come) someday. They simply didn't believe he would be God incarnate or that his name would be Jesus.

My parents never understood that their concepts and expectations concerning the Messiah were not exactly biblical. In the first place, Dad didn't believe in certain supernatural aspects—for example, that a virgin could conceive or that God could come to us in the flesh. Yet he accepted certain other Jewish traditions that were just as contrary to "the laws of nature."

For example, he once asked, "Son, do you know why Jews bury their dead in simple wooden boxes and use no metal such as nails?" Before I could reply, he continued, "Because when the Messiah returns, Jews who have died can easily kick the sides out of their coffins and crawl underneath the bedrock to Jerusalem and see him."

I said, "Dad, if you believe all that, why is the concept of a virgin becoming supernaturally pregnant so difficult for you, if God had wanted to do such a thing?"

His "last word" was always the same: "Charles, why are you always trying to convert me?" Never mind if he had been the one to initiate the subject! That would be the end of it.

And so it went. Dad would bring up a traditional question about Judaism or Christianity; I would answer him from the Scriptures. If he didn't like my answer, or in some cases my question, he would play the "convert" card and the discussion would be over—until next time. He kept asking and I believe he loved arguing about it.

When Dad really wanted to "stir the pot," he'd call my sister in New York and find a way to mention that, "Charles has been trying to convert me again." Afterward, I'd receive a somewhat indignant phone call from Barbara, telling me to "lay off Dad." Of course, her Barg genetics prompted her to volunteer a few thoughts of her own regarding her disdain for "religion" in general and Christianity in particular.

I never apologized for sharing the gospel with my dad. I told him, "Think about it Dad. I believe with all my heart that the only way to have peace with God and eternal life with him is through the Messiah, Y'shua (Jesus). If I genuinely believe that to be true and don't share it with you, my own father, then I would not be a good son at all but a wicked, selfish son."

He had no response to that, but pursed his lips in thought for a few moments before changing the subject.

In times when Dad lay critically ill, he didn't have the luxury of his armchair "safe" philosophies. As the expression goes, "There are no atheists on a burning airplane." That's when Dad did more listening than speaking, his searching eyes seeming to hope for something. Each day after work, I would stroll over to his hospital room and talk to him for hours. At those times, he was no longer the father trying to dispel the foolish notions of a son whose ideas did not square with his own worldview.

Sometimes we only consider God when hope fails. Dad's hope failed him one layer at a time. He seemed willing, when he was in a crisis, to consider what the Bible says. Then when he was well enough to feel more in control, his skepticism returned.

I always asked his permission to pray for him and to read the Psalms to him; he always replied with a simple, "Okay." I would read to him and pray for him, usually holding his hand or his head in my hands. He would close his eyes and appear to be comforted. He seemed disappointed if I was in a hurry and neglected this aspect of our visit.

Dad insisted that he did not fear death, and maybe he didn't. Yet at certain critical points during his long illness, I saw unmistakable fear and uncertainty in his eyes.

Each of us must face the ultimate hour; the moment when we discover the truth about whatever it is that we believe. Were we right or were we wrong? The Bible says we will all stand before God and give an account of ourselves someday.

At some level, most of us probably realize that truth, if not intellectually, then deep in our *kishkes*, our "gut." Perhaps that explains the sudden fear and uncertainty we all experience about death at one time or another. It seems to come from nowhere in particular; sometimes it surprises us, overtakes us with a shock of uncertainty or fear and is gone as quickly as it came. Many people try to offset or "outrun" the feeling by busying themselves about the home or office, catching up on unfinished projects and indulging various pleasures and passions—anything to keep from being alone with that feeling.

Dad and I often talked about death. He wanted to know *all* the details the Bible could offer on the subject. One evening, while frightened and near death, he admitted, "Even if I knew it (the gospel) was true, I can't do it, Son."

Surprised by his candor, I asked, "How can that possibly be? How can you know something is true, yet not embrace it for yourself?"

"Because," he continued, "I would be letting my mother and father down. When I'm really worried, I sometimes pray to them to help me." Such was his belief.

When someone admits that even the truth will not change his mind, there is nothing more to say.

I think that many people are just like my dad. They may actually believe the Bible gives real explanations for the ultimate questions of life, sin and death; but if they don't admit it to themselves or others, they somehow feel released from the responsibility of acting on those realities.

If we refuse to notice that God has expectations, do those expectations cease to exist? We can be very sensitive to the expectations of people around us, whether out of love, fear or both. Should we love or fear God any less?

Dad's personal philosophy on death and afterlife is difficult to define. Sometimes he would say, "Afterlife isn't really all that important; Jews don't worry about such things." He maintained that Jewish people concern themselves with making a good name in this life; in so doing, their eternal rewards are in the legacies they leave behind. The ideas that "when you're dead you're dead" and "only your memory lives on" are common among many Jewish people with whom I've spoken over the years.

At other times—as when Dad prayed to his departed parents for help in times of need—he did so with all certainty that his prayers were being received somewhere outside the dimensions of life as we know it. When my sister survived a train wreck down in Mexico some years ago, Dad concluded that his departed mother's spirit had saved her.

Probably, like most people, Dad had never carefully examined exactly what he believed. And like many, the reason or consistency he would exercise in business and other areas of life somehow seemed an unnecessary burden to apply to the spiritual realm. Because spiritual realities are often unseen, it is easy to behave as though they are somehow controlled alternately by our lack of interest, our desires and our imagination.

And yet, there are some realities over which we have no control.

CHAPTER SEVENTEEN:

MY BROTHER

"Charles, have you got a minute to talk?" Dad's voice was strained and cracking. He had dropped by unexpectedly at the end of a busy day at the clinic. It was not unusual for Dad and Cross to show up unannounced; Dad often stopped by to kibbitz with anyone in the office who didn't look busy.

On this day in the fall of 1987, it was obvious that he was not dropping by just to pass the time of day. He was pale, his hands were shaking more than usual and his posture was slouched. He seemed to be forcing himself to look at me.

I swallowed hard and nodded for him to continue as I holstered my pen into the top pocket of my lab coat. I turned off my tape recorder.

"Charles, you have a brother you've never met!"

"What?!" I exclaimed. "What are you talking about?" My mind struggled to make sense of his words. They were the most surprising words I'd ever heard—ever!

Dad was respected as a pillar of the Forrest City community. He was so different from some men, whom everyone knew lived double lives. Dad had money and influence, but didn't flaunt it. He was handsome and athletic, but wasn't vain about it. Neither did he posture the way some men do to prove their virility. Dad was not the town philanderer. Nobody joked about him behind his back the way they did the fathers of some of my school friends, friends for whom I felt sad because of their reckless dads' behavior. My dad wasn't like that.

My dad was the one you called if you wanted to get a job done and have it done right, without undue fanfare. He helped sponsor a Little League baseball team for the city's first season so that I would have a baseball experience. He was our city's Cub Scout master for several years and he taught us boys Marine Corps caliber calisthenics, gymnastics and precision drilling. He was president of many civic clubs. He donated his time and resources to almost anyone who called on him. He stayed away from the local nightclubs and bars. All my friends knew and respected that he was a family man first and foremost. Some even told me how much they admired him for that. For a small town, Forrest City had quite a reputation for its nightlife. Sometimes when I was out with my friends, we "happened upon" some of their fathers doing things they should not have been doing. Although my friends made light of it, I could sense their shame.

But not *my* Dad! When I was younger, we would be driving along, down some highway to anywhere, and Dad would remind me of the importance of a good reputation. He would tell me about how he worked hard to live a life that would not cause his family to be ashamed of him. He wanted me to be proud of him and I was. I still am. I knew he wasn't perfect, but it never crossed my mind that he could be unfaithful to Mom, much less be the father of a brother whom I had never met.

We both stared at the floor. After a long silence, he continued, "His name is Mark. I just met him a few months ago, and he's a very nice young man. I can't keep this from you so I'm telling you face to face." Then he added, "I hope you're not too disappointed with me. I couldn't live with that." And then he told me the story.

In 1954, the year before my bar mitzvah, Dad met a young nursing student during a trip to visit his family in Little Rock. They had an affair. He told her that despite his affection for her, he was not willing to give up his family. After a short time together, they discovered she was pregnant. They discussed possibilities and she let him know that abortion was not an option for her. She moved into a Catholic home for unwed mothers until she gave birth to a fine, healthy baby boy. Being unmarried, she thought it best to give him up for adoption.

He was adopted by a couple in Fayetteville, where his father taught physics at the University of Arkansas. When Mark was three years old, they moved to Little Rock where his father had accepted a teaching position at the University of Arkansas Graduate Institute of Technology. Mark grew up in a neighborhood in southwest Little Rock; by coincidence, he lived just two blocks from where my grandfather Barg was living.

Being raised in a German family whose natural abilities were in the academics and applications of science and mathematics, he spent much of his boyhood watching the men in the family tinker with mechanical repairs for fun on free weekends. He often wondered why he was different, preferring instead to be out in the neighborhood shmoozing with friends. He had considerable people skills, and preferred human interaction to science projects. It never entered his mind that he had a Jewish heritage deeply carved into his genetic tree.

Mark was raised in the Catholic faith, where he was, for a time, an altar boy. He even considered a future in the priesthood during his youth; instead, he pursed a career in law. After completing law school in 1980, he opened a solo practice in southwest Little Rock.

When his adoptive father died a few years later, Mark became exceedingly interested in the circumstances of his origins. As an attorney, he was adept at obtaining information that others might have had difficulty acquiring.

Mark finally located his mother and they had a joyous reunion. She told him about his father and Mark located Dad as well. The decision to contact him was difficult. Mark did not want to disrupt our family. Yet, like any other boy, he wanted to know his father personally, not just know about him.

Gathering his courage, he phoned Dad one day. He identified himself and quickly added that his only intention was to meet his father. He hoped that they could spend some time together and talk—no more. Mark assured the voice on the other end of the phone that it was "okay" if he was uncomfortable with proceeding any further.

Dad was stunned. Seldom caught off guard, he needed time to collect his thoughts. Promising to call Mark back, he took his number and abruptly ended the conversation. After a day or two, he called Mark and told him "yes," he wanted to meet him.

It was obvious from the outset that they had much in common and a mutual affection quickly developed. Dad offered his family name to Mark saying, "You're my son and it is yours if you wish to take it." Mark was surprised but moved by this powerful gesture.

As a Jew, Dad treasured his family name above all. He'd always taught me that, *"A good name is to be chosen rather than great riches."* (Proverbs 22:1). Even though my father made mistakes, he always had this ideal firmly in the crosshairs of his life's telescope. He could not have offered Mark a more valued gift. At the same time, he feared what disclosure might do to that name in the eyes of the rest of our family.

Dad finished the story, then he looked away and added, "I've tried to live my life in such a way so as to not make my family ashamed, but I've made mistakes. Just because I made a mistake is no reason for me to make another by turning my back on my son Mark, who wanted to find me after all these years. I'm willing to accept the responsibility for my actions."

He raised his head to look me directly in the face, "Are you comfortable meeting Mark?" he asked. "Because if you're not, it's okay; I understand."

I heard my mouth say, "Yes," even though my mind had not recovered from the shock. I was filled with simultaneous astonishment, curiosity, expectation, anxiety, fear and other emotions that I can't describe. I do, however, vividly remember that anger and disappointment were not among them. I nodded my head. Dad stood up slowly, took a deep breath, then left my office to get Mark, who was waiting outside in the parking lot.

Minutes later, I was looking into the face of a young man whose features and mannerisms were identical to a thirty-three year old Louis Barg. I was strangely excited, yet I knew that things would never be the same again; the status quo was about to experience a major shift. Mother would eventually find out and it would prove painful and difficult for her. Our family life, in some ways, was going to be completely transformed.

I went home and told Linda what had happened, and then I wept. I felt strangely grateful to God for giving me a brother. And my respect for my father remained strong.

Dad knew that he had opened a door that could never be closed. His human frailties exposed, life was going to be uncomfortable for him at a time when his health was failing and he needed all the love, respect and support that his family could provide. Yet he'd stepped out in courage.

It was vintage Dad. Once again, he'd responded appropriately to a very difficult situation, albeit, one of his own making.

I was proud of the way my father handled the situation. We *all* make mistakes, some of which are very serious. It's not whether we make mistakes that reveals our character; it's the way we deal with them. Do we apologize, take responsibility for a wrong done? Or do we deny our shortcomings by blaming others? Do we try to look good or to be "right" by justifying our wrongs? My father dealt with his mistakes honestly, setting a good example for me.

Dad and I did not always agree on what was right—as evidenced by his initial response to my marriage and my faith. But he had taught me to do what is right regardless of the personal cost.

CHAPTER EIGHTEEN:

A COINCIDENCE?

"Now Mark, don't try talking to your brother about that kind of stuff. He's real religious."

Dad had warned Mark that he'd get nowhere with me in a discussion that had anything to do with God. I think he probably knew that it wasn't a matter of mere religion for me; he knew that my whole life had changed because of—well, something. From my perspective, it was my relationship with God. Dad probably found that concept somewhat "out of the box" of his regular thinking, so he relegated my conversation, behavior and rapidly growing body of knowledge into the catchall of "religious."

About a year after I'd announced my belief in Jesus—when he realized that my commitment was firm—Dad acknowledged to me his observation that this faith was changing my life for the better. Sometimes he'd call to ask me a theological question so that he could relay the answer to a friend. I believe he was genuinely intrigued by the Christian doctrine of salvation through Jesus and the prospect of eternal existence with God. Sometimes late at night, I would visit him to find that he was completely absorbed by some Christian preacher on television.

Dad had actually come to be a little proud of his son the Christian, because he could see that I was still a Jew—in fact, more of a Jew than I had been. Nevertheless, Dad didn't especially want his newfound son, Mark, to have to deal with my "religious eccentricities." He advised Mark not to talk to me about the Bible because I had spent a long time studying it, believed what it said and (in his estimation) could argue so well from it that I was "not even intimidated by the scholarly rabbis."

At first, Mark seemed to me to be a reproduction of Dad, even in mannerisms—though they had never been around each other. He radiated self-assurance beyond his age and he looked a whole lot more like Dad than I did: athletic build, high cheekbones, same blue eyes. He comported himself so much like Dad that I had to rethink the nature versus nurture issue. I had firmly believed that nurture (environment) had far more influence on personality than nature. Mark made me toss that bias out the window.

I observed my new brother's life, hoping to discover his spiritual inclinations. I learned that by the time Mark enrolled in college, his theological views were much like Dad's—he felt that "a little of God" was a good thing—as long as it didn't interfere with what a man wanted to do with his life. Neither did he feel the need for a personal savior.

Mark had little interest in God and he did not seem to feel any need to develop such an interest. After all, he was a bright young professional with a good track record and no reason to doubt his own ability to control his destiny. His upbringing had, as the saying goes, "inoculated" him with just enough Christianity to prevent him from "contracting the condition." I assumed that he would be even less receptive to my belief in Jesus than the rest of my family.

Dad had already warned Mark that I was "too religious"; worse, I was outspoken about what I believed. Perhaps because of all this, I was careful not to say much about my faith to Mark as we tried to get to know one another. We met several times for lunch. We came to know each other's families. I took him flying a time or two.

Some say that a "coincidence" is a situation where God chooses to remain anonymous. Shortly after Mark and I began getting to know one another, a few such coincidences converged. First, we had a snowstorm in Little Rock. We don't get many of those in the South, so when heavy snow falls, everything grinds to a halt. Human sickness, however, does not respect weather conditions; I still had to plow my way to work to make daily hospital rounds and to be available for those few souls with 4-wheel drive vehicles who might manage to make it to the office.

This day, "coincidentally" no one showed up—except Mark. He called and told me he was out "playing" in the snow. After a bit of chatting, he came to the point and said he needed to talk. Minutes later, he was at the office. He seated himself on the same couch where Dad had first announced that I had a brother.

There was something different about Mark that day. I was accustomed to seeing him walk with his chin up, as though he were surveying the world to see if it met with his approval. While I liked Mark, it always seemed there was a wall that would prevent us from connecting on a meaningful level. That day, however, the wall seemed down. Mark looked apprehensive, and his face also reflected something I'd not seen in him before. He looked defeated. Defeated, yet like he was hoping for something—something I might be able to help him find.

We began with the usual superficialities. I asked him how work was going, and what was happening in his life. He responded on the usual social level, but soon ventured into deeper territory. I knew that Mark had a stressful law practice and a young marriage. I didn't know that his life was in crisis. Leaning solely upon his own abilities, he'd found dark storm clouds beginning to gather around his marriage and professional career.

He spoke of difficulties that discouraged him, even made him feel disconnected from life. He talked about how his marriage was not working well anymore—and how important it was to him not to have two failed marriages. He spoke openly and honestly of his uncertainty, fear and insecurity.

He told me his life was missing something. Though he was raised Catholic he didn't know anything about a personal relationship with God, didn't know what would happen to him when he died, didn't know if God could make a difference in his life.

Finally, I replied to my brother's statements. "Mark, what's missing from your life is Jesus. That's why you are feeling this way. Wouldn't you like to know that you know what God has for you?"

Mark looked down at the floor, and when he looked up he admitted, "Charles, whatever you have, I want it too. I know that you are a Christian. I want to know more about how you came to believe in Jesus!"

"Well that sure breaks the ice," I thought. "Brother, do I have something to share with you!"

I explained my spiritual journey, and how God had continued to pursue me even when I was too ignorant and arrogant to acknowledge his existence. I told him how Jesus had changed my life and Linda's life, and later on, our children's lives. I told him how God had guaranteed me complete forgiveness and eternal life.

Moments later, I moved toward Mark and asked, "Is this what you want for yourself?"

He looked me directly in the eye, his expression softening as I took his hand. "Yes, I want that," he answered. I explained that receiving salvation in Jesus is not just a matter of saying the right prayer—it's opening one's heart to God, admitting one's sin and need for forgiveness and believing that it is possible because of what Jesus did. Being serious about forgiveness also means a desire to turn from sin, and to a life that God is waiting to help you lead.

Courageously, without hesitation Mark asked Y'shua to come into his life, to be his savior and Lord, to forgive his sins and wash him white as the new snow outside.

I looked into my brother's face again. The look of defeat was gone, as were many of the tension lines. He looked peaceful, like a person who has experienced something liberating down in his very core.

I witnessed my own brother move from a life of spiritual bankruptcy that had defeated him most of his life, to spiritual newness of life. I was amazed at how perfectly God had arranged the time and the circumstances for Mark. Mark's wife Kathy eventually became a believer as well.

I waited a few months to tell Dad what had happened. He appeared to remain placid, as if it didn't matter, but I could "sense" his disappointment. Mark spoke about his faith at length with Dad some 6-12 months later as the two of them drove together to Osceola, Arkansas. During that conversation, Dad listened politely, then admitted to Mark what he could never tell me.

He said, "Mark, what you say is probably true, but even if it is, I can't change. All my life, my parents and friends have all been Jewish. My whole life has been built around Judaism. I would lose my friends and family if I were to believe like you and Charles do. It's too late for me to change!"

The truth is, Jewish men and women far older than my dad have taken that "leap" only to find that they are as Jewish as ever, regardless of what others may think or say. As courageous as my father was all his life, he couldn't seem to see that fear of change could rob him of the most precious gift of all.

Since that time, my brother and I have become the best of friends—we have owned an airplane together, taught children's Sunday school together, prayed for each other in difficult times and watched God do great things in each other's lives.

My dad had brought Mark and me into each other's lives—but God alone is a heavenly Father who can unite sons with their earthly fathers and link brother to brother despite circumstances that have alienated them. He chose something as mundane as a snowstorm to make Mark and me brothers forever.

CHAPTER NINETEEN:

GRIEF

"Charles! I'm *okay*!" Dad spoke sharply to me through his pain. He was exasperated by my concern and desperate to avoid another trip to the hospital.

"No Dad, you are *not* okay." I could diagnose what had happened from ten yards away. Dad had grown so thin that it was painfully apparent that his femur was protruding in one direction, his hip socket in another. He continued to contradict me, insisting he had merely bruised himself. I knew very well this might be the final blow that would end up taking his life.

***

During those last years, Dad usually seemed fully aware that he was reaching the end of his life. Mom fed him plenty of vitamins and consulted several homeopathic medicine sources. He tried to "humor" her by following along. Sometimes, Mom secretly consulted mystics who promised healing through their ancient "arts." She was determined to keep trying when no one else seemed to have any acceptable answers. Alas, predictably, neither did they!

Dad told me that he didn't really believe in "all that stuff," yet he could let himself be persuaded for short periods of time, of this or that new cure. Like most of us, I guess he found that "desperate times call for desperate measures," including unconventional alternatives. It was not unusual to see Dad tagging along with Mom to visit the latest "expert." After each visit, he couldn't wait to update me on whatever naturalist treatment strategy he had learned. Sometimes he'd insist that I begin incorporating this or that new discovery into my own medical practice without delay.

At Mother's insistence, Dad hastened to employ various vitamin and "compost poultice" strategies. Yet he essentially ignored advice/instruction about basic good health realities regarding medication schedules, proper diet and daily exercise.

At times, Dad was not lucid and Mom was unable to manage his care, but both of them refused to consider a nursing home. Dad's diabetes had taken away most of the strength and sensation from his lower extremities. He disregarded my advice and not only walked unassisted up and down stairs, but he would motor out each morning onto busy boulevards in Little Rock just to visit his favorite restaurant and have breakfast with his buddies. These buddies often told me how amazed they were to look out and see his car inching up to the handicapped spot—his "spot"—day after day.

Dad's well muscled legs now looked like skin covered bones, that's how thin and frail he had become. He almost looked like the Holocaust survivors you see leaving the camps in some of the old newsreels. Some of his friends doubted that he would be able to survive for another week, expecting each breakfast to be their last time together.

One day, the inevitable happened; Dad fell and broke his hip. He tried to convince me that he had only suffered a minor injury, a bruise. And certainly a huge bruise had covered his skin with frightening speed. But his obviously distorted anatomy indicated worse problems. As I lifted him off the floor to carry him to my car, I knew he understood his left hip was broken. Nevertheless he assured me, "It will be okay in a few days."

After his hip surgery, Dad became very confused and disoriented. Mom felt terribly guilty about not being able to manage him at home. She could not admit to herself or to any of us that he had become too much to handle.

I'd watched Dad care for his own aging father and knew he'd had to make difficult decisions. Dad had raised me to be strong and decisive, like he was. I knew that in his better moments he would want to spare Mom the trauma of trying (and failing) to care for him when the severity of his condition so far exceeded her abilities.

In one of the most difficult decisions of my life, I admitted Dad to a nearby nursing home. He never knew how I cried when the nurse from the home called me for his admission orders.

Every day, Dad would call me at the office and plead with me to get him out of there, back home to Mom. Sometimes after these conversations I would disappear into my private office for a little while, cry, pray, compose myself and ask God to continue to give me the courage and strength to do what was right, even though it was painful.

I knew that Dad would want me to do what needed to be done, and do it like the man he had purposed for me to be. My father had given me the understanding and courage to do what was necessary, but I had to come repeatedly to my heavenly Father in order to renew the strength I needed to "keep on keeping on." In a sense, between "two fathers" I was able to do what needed to be done.

So when Dad called daily and pleaded with me to liberate him, I planted my feet firm and stayed the course. Every evening I would visit Dad to spend time with him, but also to evaluate him, check his chart and monitor his progress in physical rehabilitation. The reports were always the same; he was completely uncooperative and was not even attempting to bear weight on his recovering limb.

One night when the phone rang I braced myself for the usual outpouring of pleas begging me to get him "out of this place where everyone is real old and there is nothing for me to do!" He usually tried to convince me that he would do just as well at home and insisted that he would not be a burden to Mom. That night, however, was different.

In a gentle, fully lucid voice, Dad said, "Son, I know that this is hard on you and that you have tough decisions to make about me. I just want you to know that I know you love me and that you're doing what you have to do. Now go get some rest and try not to work yourself to death the way I did."

Those words were more uplifting than any other words he had ever uttered to me. How often I had pretended, "I don't need Dad's approval or his recognition and affirmation of my goals, labors and achievements." The effect his words had on me that night proved that even when the roles were reversed, I still longed for his approval.

His mind eventually began to clear as the infection subsided and his diabetes, fluid and electrolyte status improved. Still, it was clear that his death was imminent. If not diabetes, then progressive kidney failure, which claimed his own father's life, would soon surely claim his life too.

We made a family decision to convert a bedroom at his condominium into a hospital room. When it was finished, the room was filled with medical support devices to assist with comfort care. We hired part-time nurses to provide full-time medical and nutritional support, thus relieving Mom of the burden while enabling Dad to spend the rest of his life at home with her. Everything we needed was at our fingertips, including catheters, IV set ups, IV medication, a hospital bed with trapeze, a lift chair, oxygen—everything!

I made bedside rounds twice a day, administering and adjusting Dad's medication as needed. One day he would be volume depleted with worsening kidney failure, so I'd have to increase his fluids; the next day he would be volume overloaded, in congestive heart failure and in need of urgent fluid removal. It was a continuous tightrope walk with constant care and attention needed. When I wasn't there during the daytime and late at night, the nurses were my eyes and ears.

This continued for many, many weeks; it's called the graveyard spiral. It occurs when a person's condition waxes and wanes in response to fluid challenge until eventually, he lapses into a deep stupor, the heart straining to beat one more time.

We expected each day to be Dad's last; then he'd wake up, look around and ask for water or soup. Amazingly, he sometimes talked to us in brief, comprehensible phrases—and even stunned us with an occasional, very appropriate funny comment, just as he had for so many years.

Dad was the bravest man I ever knew. He had courage for life and for death. He once told me that a brave man is not one who never knows fear; such a man is not brave at all—he is merely a fool. He said that a brave man is a man who is realistic about his fears, counts the cost and moves past his fears to do what is right anyway, whether it's to live or to die. That makes a lot more sense to me now looking back on his life. He had his moments of fear, but fear did not control his life.

All of his life, Dad had prepared me for his death. He knew it would come someday, and as with everything else, he wanted me to know exactly how to handle everything at that time.

By now, Linda was sitting up with Dad all night. She would feed him, clean him and place his *yarmulke* atop his head. She would sing Yiddish songs to him, the way his mother used to do. When she left his bedside for a moment, he would sense it and become restless, then start calling out for his mother or his sister Ethyl.

Finally, one morning I arrived about 6:00 a.m. "Good morning, Mom. How'd you sleep?" I asked.

"I slept unusually sound last night," she said. (For months, she had been sleeping very restlessly as Dad usually called out to her in the night to come and be at his bedside.) "Last night, your dad suddenly became more alert. Instead of asking me to be near his bedside, or crying out for me in the night, he asked the nurse to tell me to go to bed and to get a good night's sleep. Your father said that he would be okay by himself!" She seemed greatly encouraged by that.

We entered his bedroom together. The only sound in the room was the oxygen flowing from the canister into Dad's unmoving chest. He was gone! I moved quickly to his side to feel his last few heartbeats. His pupils were dilated and fixed. Mom didn't recognize that Dad had left us. We both stood there in silence for several minutes. I wept silently, carefully planning each word that Mom would need to hear.

"What's the matter, Charles?" Mom was smiling weakly toward Dad. "He must have gotten a good night's rest because I didn't hear him at all last night. Is something wrong?"

I went to Mom and put one arm around her, looking slowly and deeply into her eyes. I didn't have to say a thing, she knew. She moved closer to him, at first not believing; then she leaned over onto his lifeless body and cried out, "Louis, don't leave me! I need your strength!" We held each other and wept together for a long time.

We all needed Dad's strength—Mom, me, my sister Barbara, our children, everyone else whose life he had touched. Each of us drew life from him. Even with his flaws, he was our anchor. He was Dad; he loved each of us in a special way, and he gave us his life. What more can a man give to those he loves?

After what seemed like hours, I asked Mom if she would leave the room so I could spend a few minutes alone with him. I kissed his face and spoke to him in a new language—a communication of the heart that sons and fathers long to express to one another but seldom do, until one day the opportunity no longer exists. It's a tragedy that is too often passed on from generation to generation.

I know Dad loved me. He told me so and proved it many times in his own way of expressing devotion to me. Yes, he did it his way, but he did it and I knew it. Still, there was a level of intimacy missing. How easy it is for us men to settle for only a shadow of what could be. If only we weren't so afraid to admit needs that we fear would make us appear weak in the other person's eyes.

In the same way, many of us long for a relationship with our heavenly Father, only to discover at the end of our days that all we had was a sliver of a shadow of what might have been. Why don't we just drop the pretense and run to him?

How often do people hear, and perhaps even repeat, that God is a crutch, or that religion is for the weak? Pride prevents us from seeking the one solution to the human problem because we don't want to appear weak. It keeps us from admitting our failures, or if we do admit them, it keeps us from admitting that what we need most is something we'll never be able to earn or deserve—because that's what a relationship with God is.

I'm not talking about the kind of pride that expresses itself as pleasure in a job done well. Rather, it's the pride that expresses itself in *dis*pleasure at the idea that we need God—much less that we can only have a relationship with him on his terms. It's the pride that says, "It's my way or the highway."

That type of pride brings us down. From its epicenter spring crippling emotions: jealousy, anger, self-centeredness, strife, broken promises, fragmented lives and every manner of indignity that human beings force one another to endure. It is a vicious cycle that affects all relationships.

Yet God provided all we need to have an amazing relationship with him, which in turn, sheds light on our relationships with others. Though God is holy and we are not, he bridged the gap between us by sending the Messiah as an atonement for our sin. He calls us to cross that bridge but if we don't accept that he is calling, or we refuse the bridge he has provided for us, we remain far from him.

Dad blessed me by setting high standards, albeit standards which even he himself could not attain. Throughout his lifetime, he challenged me to love what is right. Through him I first learned of morality, responsibility, loyalty, fairness, charity, family and many other things that I have attempted to describe in this writing. If my father had not attempted to achieve and maintain his standards, my life would surely be a rather ghostly story, truly a life without hope.

Dad always did the best he knew how for me. Sometimes that meant trying to override my choices when he thought I was wrong. But he also inculcated enough backbone in me so that I could do what I knew was right, even when he didn't support me.

It is said that the true sign of maturity is the ability to forgive one's parents. No matter how much I love and respect Dad, I had my disappointments and pain over some of his shortcomings—as I am sure my children have had and will have with me.

There are no perfect parents, apart from our heavenly Father. The great thing about God is that he not only wants what is best for us, but he truly understands what that is. Yet he does not coerce us into choosing what is best. When we are ready to trust him, to believe that he is the source of what is true and right, and to set aside our own preconceptions, he will help us make the right choices.

I wish with all my heart that Dad had that kind of trust in God. Like most people, he would not embrace certain ideas, even truths, because he feared those he loved (even those no longer living) would reject him.

I cannot simply "wish" Dad into God's presence, nor can I rationalize that everything's "okay" simply because he's my father. Jesus said, "I am the way, the truth, and the life. *No one* comes to the Father except through Me" (John 14:6, emphasis added).

Only God knows the final destiny of my father, as well as the love that I hold for him. All my wishing will not change the result. Many have said, "How can you believe something that denies the eternal security of your own father if he did not believe as you do?" The answer is, my personal happiness is not the basis on which something is or isn't true. Therefore, it should not be the basis for what I believe.

Each of us will stand before a holy God someday and have to account for our own choices—and whether or not we wanted to know God's truth or refused to hear it because it did not please us or we feared what others would think.

I love Dad, miss him, think about him every day and want to be with him in the next life; but I never saw evidence that Dad gave his life to the Messiah Jesus. I cannot twist God's written revelation just to appease my own grief.

Therefore, I will rest in that tension, trusting my heavenly Father with the outcome, with thankfulness in my heart for him having given me 54 years with a father who loved me and who proved it to me again and again over the course of our lives together on this planet.

CHAPTER TWENTY:

FROM BEYOND THE GRAVE

"Oy-yoy, Yoy-yoy, yoy-yoy, Yoyyyyy."

My head was filled with the rhythmic, almost mystical, wailing cadence of my grandparents as I emerged from the deep enveloping shroud of anesthesia.

Then I heard a different voice that seemed to belong to someone whose hand firmly held my shoulder. "Charles, your margins are clear! You will never die of prostate cancer!" Dr. Greene spoke firmly, personally—with kindness.

"What is he talking about," I wondered. "Where am I?" Then I felt the pain, burning and penetrating deep within my abdomen.

I looked down through glazed visual fields to see what appeared to be a long bandage from mid-abdomen to the extent of my lower parts.

My surgery had lasted four and a half hours. Normally, a radical prostatectomy takes half that time, but Dr. Graham Greene, the brilliant and perfectionist Nova Scotian had been careful to separate, examine and send directly to pathology every gram of tissue—thus making sure he left nothing of malignant potential inside me.

As vision in my solitary eye began to clear somewhat, it began to come back to me. I could see and smell the activity in the recovery room. I shut my eyes and tried to remember Dr. Greene's reassuring words as I drifted off to sleep.

Hours later, I awoke in a private room with tubes going everywhere and familiar faces on all sides, watching and waiting for me to interact. There was Linda, my beautiful wife smiling gently as she kissed my forehead and moved to comfort me. All the children and grandchildren were gathered at the foot of the bed, smiling broadly toward me as if to say "Dad, we love you. We know you have gone through a lot, but you are going to be okay." Friends from church as well as people I hadn't seen in years were knocking at the door and were ushered into the room until the room could hold no more people.

I tried to think of something funny to say—to put everyone at rest and let them know I was okay. I knew that Linda and the children would continue to worry until they heard me say something on the lighthearted side.

But something was missing. What was it? The experience felt so familiar, so *deja vu*, and yet, something was very different. Then I remembered. I'd only been in this position once before. Fifty-three years earlier—the last time I saw a surgical table, a recovery room, and smelled the anesthesia, a strong yet gentle hand was upon my shoulder—it was Dad!

He was the only one there, to love me, encourage me, care for me. Just him and me. "That is what's missing—dear God, my father is gone!" The thought exploded in my head. I began to weep.

It was obvious that no one in the room understood my tears. No one even asked. This was a freeze-frame moment that I needed, between me, the Father, and memories of my Dad. I drifted off into a deep, restful sleep knowing that even after my father was gone, his love and care had probably saved my life.

It began with a patient's large sebaceous cyst about one to two centimeters in diameter. He was sitting on the examining table with his back to me, the cyst on his neck red and swollen—more than ripe enough for an incision and drainage procedure. I gently inserted the needle of the syringe, filled with xylocaine, beneath the epidermis, and injected a small amount of local anesthetic. The sudden increase of pressure within the cyst caused it to rupture violently into my face.

I stopped for a moment to wash myself and re-sterilize the area; then I continued the procedure. After removing the cyst and packing the wound with iodoform gauze, I sent my patient home on oral antibiotics.

In twenty-three years of practice, this was the first time I had contaminated myself during a procedure. The nurse assistants were quick to remind me that I must comply with OSHA standards and have my blood analyzed for HIV and hepatitis viruses. They had already followed procedure by obtaining some of the patient's blood before he left the office.

I wasn't particularly fearful of the results—after all, the patient "looked okay." However, as "the boss," it was up to me to set the example and follow procedure, so I complied with the protocol. The nurse drew my blood and I went about the day's usual business, which included seeing about 45-50 patients, problem-solving here and there.

As I passed by the lab room that evening, I happened to glance down at my lab slip. I noticed that additional blood tests that I had not requested were ordered, including a blood sugar, lipid profile and a PSA (prostate specific antigen). The latter is used as a marker for the possible presence of prostate cancer in men.

Like most doctors, I don't particularly like being a patient. Whether it is due to fear, because of my childhood experience of losing an eye, or a control issue, I'm not sure. At first, I was a little upset with my nurse and asked who had ordered labs on me without my permission.

Nobody admitted to it, until finally, after some low level "brow beating" Angie, the office manager, stepped forward and confessed. I reminded her that she had overstepped her boundaries and I lectured her quite thoroughly. Unfazed by my criticism, she gently reminded me that it had been a long time since I had visited my doctor—actually I'd only done so twice in twenty-three years—and she thought it was past time for me to have routine screening blood work. I looked at her in disbelief, snatched the requisition slip and crossed out items that I did not feel were necessary, specifically the PSA test.

Angie had lost her father shortly after she came to work for me in 1990. My wife and I had come to love her as our own daughter. Now, here she was, arms folded, posturing assertively in my face. Her expression was so uncharacteristic as she stared at me like flint, letting me know that she had no intention of letting me off the hook. After retreating to my office for a moment, I relented, but only to appease her. I reluctantly walked back to the nurse's station and instructed them to reorder the tests I'd just deleted.

Two days later, the PSA result came back: 11.5 (normal is 0-4.0). I had suffered from prostatitis for years, so I didn't expect my PSA to be normal. I figured the number was probably elevated because I had suffered a particularly severe case of prostatitis just six weeks earlier, while out in Colorado with my son on a ski trip.

But 11.5 is not a number to be ignored! Without delay, I called a friend, a urology specialist, and asked his advice. He advised me to treat myself with appropriate antibiotics for four weeks, then to recheck the PSA. He also invited me upstairs for a digital prostate examination. If the PSA were to return to normal, then everything would probably be okay. If not, then I would need to have a prostate ultrasound and biopsy.

After four weeks, the PSA had barely decreased. The doctor performed a prostate ultrasound and biopsy on me, which revealed a very large prostate, chronic prostatitis and *prostate cancer*!

I was stunned. The pathologist reported that this malignancy produced a Gleason's Score of 7, which is somewhat aggressive, but not the worst report one can have. Another year or so of neglect and it may have been quite a different story.

I gathered all the office employees together so I could tell them about my illness and express my appreciation for their faithfulness and loyalty to me these many years. Then I looked at Angie, who was weeping, and thanked her for being so "stubborn." I commented that she had perhaps saved my life because I wouldn't have found out about the cancer had it not been for her. Her reply took me totally off guard.

"Doctor Barg," she said softly, "I had to do it. Your dad came by the office to talk to me shortly before his death. He used to worry about you all the time, and was afraid that you would neglect your own health. He made me promise him that I would make you get yourself checked, and that I would not let you talk me out of it. It was time to keep my word to him; I couldn't let him down!"

Her words struck deep, deep down inside me. Three years after my father's death, his love and care could still make all the difference.

Later that evening, as my car slipped quietly along the freeway toward home, my mind was immersed in a deep reflection. Glancing in the mirror, I noticed that my facial expression was fixed at a half-smile, the kind one wears when something has suddenly surfaced from one's subconscious. I nodded my head in delight to no one in particular.

The boulevard scenery produced serial memory prods, which seemed to leap to life, reminding me of Dad's life. "Over there is the little restaurant that Dad liked so much!" "There is a low flying airplane over the I-430 river bridge!" "That gray Oldsmobile is just like Dad's; there's a young man driving it and an old man sitting at his side, talking to him—they are smiling!"

And then I heard myself saying, "Thank you Dad—thank you!" My Dad's loving influence had once again embraced and protected me. And once again, it gave me life!

POSTSCRIPT

I wrote this manuscript six months after my radical prostate operation for prostate cancer and six weeks after a total thyroid removal surgery. I consider it a horrible way to lose weight. I would not recommend it to anyone, particularly if they know of a better way!

All of the post-op reports and prognoses are encouraging to this point. My doctors are telling me I am "cured." Certainly, I am excited about that. Through it all, God was there for me. He provided me the grace to take each awkward step. My heavenly Father literally walked me through the whole ordeal, so that I am able to report, firsthand, that his grace is sufficient!

Now, everyone is telling me how "great I look." It reminds me of one of Dad's favorite observations. He used to chuckle and say, "My son, there are only three stages of life: young, middle-age and "Boy, you sure look great!"

I guess the "young" part flew by pretty fast, though, not surprisingly, my memories of youth are more vivid than those of middle age.

It seems like yesterday that my tenth grade English teacher, Mrs. Bridgeforth, encouraged me to write. She was a soft-spoken, patient, middle-aged woman with a kind face. She was the very first teacher who ever looked at me with "believing" eyes. I do not know why to this day. I was a hopeless daydreamer whose mind was always fixed on some great "elsewhere." Nevertheless, one time in class, she said to me, "Oh Charles, you write so nicely!" I knew that, if ever there was a story inside me, I would someday write it all down.

Years later, after dropping out of my first year of college, I came home and decided to write a book. My heart was bursting with youthful emotions: of heroes and ambitions and life. After spending three days in my bedroom pecking away on my old "Hunton" typewriter, wasting countless paper balls for waste-basketball fodder, I gave up.

I can still see my father quietly opening my bedroom door to bring me a snack during those disappointing days. He'd pat me knowingly on the shoulder; then he would slip, just as quietly, back out the door. In retrospect, I think he knew what I was too immature to know: *My meager life's experiences had not provided me with anything to say!*

Some forty years later, I finally had something to say. Now, Dad is no longer merely in my thoughts, he is on the printed page; alive and once again larger than life. Writing about our lives prompted me to consider his fatherhood in retrospect. I could never adequately appreciate it while he was here. What a tragedy that is!

My father! The very thought of him is bittersweet. It is good to remember him. It is healing.

Thank you for taking this journey with me. I hope that if you have not already, you too, will find grace and healing from the outstretched hand of your heavenly Father, who eagerly waits for you, offering forgiveness and salvation through his Son!

It used to frustrate me that my father seemed to require me to prove my love by a lifetime of complete devotion to his plan for my life. His plans were not always perfect, did not always take into account who I was. And yet, in some way, I can understand that there is a sense in which a father's plan for his son was meant to be perfect, and that the son would show his love through obeying that plan.

I am talking about Jesus, whose love was proven by a lifetime of complete devotion to his Father's plan. And while my own devotion to my heavenly Father's plan for me is far from perfect, I have seen that his plans for me are good, that they involve real choices and reaching my best potential. An earthly father cannot be perfect in his plans or expectations but our heavenly Father is. And our obedience to him is the best way to love God, ourselves and others, since we have so much to gain and so much to give by living according to that plan.

I realize that my father provided me with a framework for understanding and appreciating God as the Father of all. Dad was a good model. I understand that there are many who grew up, either without a father, or with one who was far from being a good model. For some readers, the idea of God as Father is a fearful, if not repugnant concept.

If you haven't had a good framework for understanding a father's love as it should be, may I suggest that you take a moment and ask God to help you understand what he wants you to know about his love and care for you?

God is truly a Father to the fatherless! Will you ask him to adopt you into his family; to receive you, take your sin away, embrace you and protect you? Will you ask him to be your Father, and to show you his perfect plans for a life that will not only challenge you to reach your potential, but will give you peace and joy and purpose?

If you have not already done so, there is no better time than right now! Who knows what surprises tomorrow may hold for each of us? The only really insurmountable tragedy that life can impose on any of us is to awaken and find that the clock of time has run down, leaving us Fatherless for all of eternity!

WHAT WILL YOU DO?

If you believe that true well-being comes from God, and if you want that peace and well-being, please consider the following:

1. God is concerned with every aspect of your life.
   "Yet I will not forget you. See, I have inscribed you on the palms of My hands" (Isaiah 49:15–16).
2. You can't truly experience God's love because of sin.
   "But your iniquities have separated you from your God; and your sins have hidden His face from you, so that He will not hear" (Isaiah 59:2).
3. Trust in God's provision of Y'shua (Jesus) to be your sin-bearer and savior.
   "But He was wounded for our transgressions, He was bruised for our iniquities; the chastisement for our peace was upon Him, and by His stripes we are healed" (Isaiah 53:5).
4. Receive forgiveness of sins and a personal relationship with God by asking Y'shua to reign in your heart.
   "If you confess with your mouth the Lord [Y'shua] and believe in your heart that God has raised Him from the dead, you will be saved. For with the heart one believes unto righteousness, and with the mouth confession is made unto salvation" (Romans 10:9-10).

If you believe these verses and want to follow Y'shua, the doctor who can heal your soul, this is a prayer that will help you begin a new life: "Dear God,

I know that I have sinned against you and I want to turn from my sin. I believe you provided Y'shua, Jesus, as an atonement for me. With this prayer I receive Jesus as my savior and my Lord. Thank you God for cleansing me of sin, for healing my soul and for sealing my name in your Book of Life forever. Please help me live the life you have for me through Messiah. Amen."

If you just prayed this prayer or if you are considering doing so, please let us hear from you by filling out and returning this coupon:

(Please print)

Name _____

Street _____

City _____ State _____ Zip _____

Phone (   ) _____

E-mail _____

❑ I read the texts from the Bible and prayed the prayer. I sign my name as a commitment to Y'shua as my savior and Lord.

Signed _____

Date _____

❑ I really don't understand or believe these texts yet but I am seriously willing to consider them and seek what God has for me.

❑ I already believe in Y'shua and want to know more about Jews for Jesus.

I am ❑ Jewish ❑ Gentile

Please return to Jews for Jesus
60 Haight Street
San Francisco, CA 94102-5895
E-mail: jfj@jewsforjesus.org
www.jewsforjesus.org

WMDECAK